Memories Of Wembley

Growing Up In The Forties & Fifties

Derek Addison & Tony Rock

*To Ray
Best Wishes
Derek Addison
2011*

Memories of Wembley

ISBN: 978-1-907540-34-9

Published March 2011
Printed and Published by Anchorprint Group Limited
www.anchorprint.co.uk

Copyright © Derek Addison & Tony Rock 2011

All rights reserved.
No part of this publication may be reproduced, stored in a retrieval system, transmitted or utilised in any form or by any means, electronic, mechanical, photocopying, recording or otherwise, without written permission from the copyright holder.

CONTENTS

INTRODUCTION	1
PREFACE	3
WEMBLEY	7
WARTIME	53
EDUCATION	71
HOME LIFE	93
BEFORE COMPUTER GAMES	107
RECREATION	127
ENTERTAINMENT	165
THE NEW GENERATION	189
ACKNOWLEDGEMENTS	215

INTRODUCTION

This book is not intended to be a history of Wembley, it is simply a collection of memories and anecdotes by two friends who lived and grew up in Wembley from the forties through to the sixties.

On the occasion of Tony's annual visit to these shores from the USA where he has lived for many years, Tony and Derek like to make a pilgrimage to the resurrected Ace Café on the North Circular Road in Stonebridge, to enjoy an excellent English Breakfast and perhaps to reminisce about their possibly misspent youth, frequenting transport cafés, coffee bars and Rock & Roll clubs over fifty years ago.

Derek now lives in Chalfont St. Peter, Bucks, a miraculously preserved village, reminiscent of the England we grew up in. Our journey to the Ace would generally take us down the Western Avenue to Hangar Hill, and then along the North Circular to Stonebridge. Apart from road improvements and the loss of a few pubs and landmark buildings, very little has changed along this route since the fifties. Our return journey would then be via Wembley High Road, and Ealing Road, where the changes have been so profound that we decided that our recollections of the Wembley we grew up in should be recorded. To do this we have to mentally turn the clock back to the twenty years from the onset of WW2, to 1960, a period that saw radical changes in society, the birth of the welfare state, and advances in technology that could only have been imagined in science fiction novels of the thirties.

In the 1940s most of the working classes were living from hand to mouth. Wartime rationing would continue after the war for a further nine years, Britain being the last western country to end rationing. A 48 hour working week was the norm, the floor covering of choice was linoleum, with fitted carpets a distant dream. However, by 1960, people had begun to have a few pounds in their pockets. An increasing number of people had cars, and almost every house boasted a television set.

Readers of a similar age to us, may be reminded of things long forgotten, and possibly be prompted to tell their grandchildren about the life they knew as children.

A wise man once observed that if ten people were asked to describe a particular event that occurred fifty years earlier, there would be at least fifteen versions. It is therefore inevitable that some of our readers will find things to disagree with. We can only repeat that this is not intended as a history, or a work of reference, and apologize for any small errors.

Derek Addison & Tony Rock 2011.

PREFACE

Before 1924 when the British Empire Exhibition first opened, Wembley as a town was almost unknown. Originally, what is now Wembley Central (renamed in 1948) railway station was marked 'Sudbury, for Wembley'. From that point in time, the progress of urbanisation was phenomenal.

Kingsbury was added to the borough in 1934, by which time Wembley was considered to be the outstanding place to live in Middlesex. From a mere 5000 in 1900, the population of the Borough had risen to 115,000 by 1940.

In October 1937, Wembley became a Borough by virtue of a Royal Charter.

During the late thirties, when speculative builders were blighting the Wembley area with countless ill-designed, and often jerry-built, semi-detached Mock Tudor houses, a number of public buildings of outstanding design were commissioned by the Wembley Council. These included three schools, Barham, Lyon Park, and Vicars Green. Also Wembley Fire Station, and of course the Wembley Town Hall, since the old council offices in the High Road, at the corner of St Johns Road were now far too small for the expanded town. The new town hall, designed by Clifford Strange, was completed just as WW2 broke out.

All of the new council projects were low level, bright and airy brick buildings, boasting the latest large, galvanized steel, Crittall window frames, and hot water central heating systems, representing the leading edge of building design at the time.

The available facilities in the new town hall included the council chamber and offices, a public assembly hall, a public library, and a bomb-proof first aid post. In 1944 the main hall was used as an assembly point for children being evacuated from the danger of the V1 flying bombs. Derek remembers waiting at this assembly point with his mother, younger sister and baby brother for evacuation to the country.

The Wembley Town Hall remains to this day a modern looking building, and over the years has been the venue for concerts, dances, boxing and wrestling matches, and more recently pop concerts.

With the re-districting of London in 1960s it became Brent Town Hall, and so it remains today.

Other examples of fine prize winning architecture in the Wembley area would include Alperton (1933) and Sudbury Town (1931) underground stations, designed by Charles Holden for the recently completed Piccadilly line. Another fine example of the period was the Alperton Bus Garage (1939).

By the time the authors were old enough to be aware of their surroundings, Wembley had completed the transition from an agricultural to an urban area. Although there were still wide swathes of undeveloped land in the area, active farming had more or less vanished by the time the war broke out, although Tony can still remember seeing cows in the back meadow of Barham Park. In those days, one didn't have to travel far outside the borough to be in real farming country. The newly built North Circular Road might be considered as the boundary, East of which was London, with older buildings dating to the late Victorian and Edwardian building booms, while West of the North Circular most of the buildings in Wembley dated from the late twenties and thirties. During our schooldays, a bicycle ride to the country, would take us to Beaconsfield, Chesham, or Amersham, which at the time was still a small market town with a surprising number of public houses on each side of its main street. The towns were still surrounded by farming country and the inhabitants still spoke with the broad Buckinghamshire accents. A trip to Rickmansworth or Watford found people with a Hertfordshire accent. This would be familiar to those who remember the Bernard Miles humorous monologues on the radio. People were at that time less inclined to move around the country, and regional accents were still very strong.

During the war, most of the remaining open land around Wembley had been ploughed up for allotment gardens, and later, those areas which were not used for post war housing development, were often abandoned, providing a habitat for countless butterflies and small birds which are seldom seen today.

As a point of pride, almost every house would have a flower garden, or at the very least a trim privet hedge and a small lawn in the front garden. Compare this with today, where nine out of ten houses in Wembley simply have an oil-stained patch of cracked concrete connecting directly to the pavement. A once well used and well maintained footpath running alongside the railway from the end of Lancelot Road to North Wembley is today rank with weeds and choked by abandoned furniture and old cooking stoves. The once carefully maintained pavements in the Borough are now in many places broken and uneven. The tall avenues of elm trees, which once graced the parks in the area were all lost in the seventies to Dutch Elm disease, and never re-planted. The classic twin towers of the Wembley Stadium, an internationally recognized symbol of the Borough were torn down in an act of manifest vandalism and replaced by a structure notable for its sheer ugliness. Had this eyesore been built in the sixties, the architect might well have been suspected of using LSD for his inspiration.

Sadly, our Wembley no longer exists. Only the memory remains…

Wembley Fire and Ambulance Station in 1955
Tony's elder Brother, ambulance driver V.J Rock, poses beside his vehicle.

WEMBLEY

PUBLIC SERVICES.

Wembley is noted for The marked sobriety of the population, the excellent sanitary condition of the houses, roads and premises. The good drainage and water supply, and the stimulating influence of keen sanitarians and practitioners, whether clerical, medical or laymen.

The Medical officer of Health, Wembley, 1939.

Generally speaking, Wembley was well provided with public services in the forties and fifties. The council road menders and their steam-roller, resurfaced the roads regularly with tar and gravel. In Autumn, the leaves from the plane trees were swept up and taken away. The dustmen came each week to empty the dustbins, and the gaslights in the side streets received regular maintenance.

It was accepted as a matter of course, that the streets and pavements would be swept by a council employee pushing a cart loaded with brooms and shovels. The universal public trait of littering at the time, and the tendency to allow dogs to run loose and foul the pavements, did nothing to make the work of these sweepers easier.

The town had an excellent little Cottage Hospital, and a District Nurse service the members of which would often be seen whisking round Wembley in their dark blue uniforms, riding their little auto-cycles.

At the start of the war, Wembley was in the fortunate position of having the greater portion of its infrastructure built less than twenty years previously. Some of the older areas still had gas lighting, but the vast number of 'Metroland' houses were modern, with full plumbing, sewage, electrical and gas supplies. The water was supplied by the Colne Valley Water Company, and sewage was discharged into the Middlesex trunk sewer to be dealt with outside the Borough. In earlier times, Wembley had a rather poor record for sewage disposal, with a sewage farm situated along Alperton Lane, often discharging raw effluent into the river Brent, a practice which was the subject of regular complaints from the Thames Conservancy.

This sewage farm was closed down and the area became the site of a first class, public cleansing department, with an incinerator for household rubbish, and a salvage plant.

Street cleaning and rubbish collection were also part of the responsibility of this facility.

During and for some time after the war, waste food was also collected around the borough and cooked into a nutritious pig food, which was sold to offset the cost of running the department.

The town gas supply was provided by the Gas Light & Coke company, who's large steam driven Sentinel trucks were often to be seen driving around the area. The showrooms of the company at 152 to 154 Wembley High Road had all the latest stoves, gas fires and water heaters on display, as well as having service facilities and a desk for the payment of gas bills, although many houses at the time still had a coin operated gas meter, which would be emptied from time to time by the company.

Electricity was provided by the North Metropolitan Company, which also had showrooms in Wembley High Road, at number 71, displaying all the latest electrical appliances.

Electric cooking stoves were not as popular as the traditional Gas stoves, and like electric fires were considered to be expensive to run. Many homes in Wembley also had coin operated electricity meters.

There was a general post office and telephone exchange in the High Road, next to the Odeon cinema, and post war, a much larger telephone exchange was built behind the post office. Telegrams could be sent from the post office, and incoming telegrams were delivered promptly by bicycle and later, motor-cycle equipped telegraph boys.

Apart from the cemetery at St Johns Church, there was a public burial ground at Clifford Road in Alperton.

In addition to the state schools there were a surprising number of small private schools in the borough, seven in Wembley alone, the largest of which,

Wembley Girls Grammar School, became Pitmans secretarial college shortly after the war.

On the Harrow Road at the corner of Ranleigh Road, stood Wembley Police station, X Division. With steps leading up to the entrance door on the corner of the building, surmounted by the customary large blue lamp. It was at the time an imposing building, with extensive garage and maintenance facilities at the rear. Built at the original level of the area, a large portion of the ground floor was below street level and could be looked down on from the pavement through the iron bar fence surrounding the building.

In the forties and fifties, the police still did foot patrols around the area, and during the war, they often set aside the regular police helmets in favour of an army style tin hat. The duty sergeant would tour the various beats, riding a heavy framed 28 inch wheel bicycle. There were blue police telephone boxes located at strategic points around the area, with direct lines to the local police station. Private telephones were not common in the forties. There was a light on top of the kiosk, switched on remotely, to attract the attention of the patrolling officer if the police station wished to contact him. The inside of the call boxes, accessible to the police but not to the public, also sometimes contained a 'Pigs Ear' urinal for the convenience of the officers. Today this type of call box would be instantly identified by children as a Tardis. With the introduction of personal mobile radio's for patrol officers in 1965, and the spread of private telephones in homes, the old police telephone boxes were finally phased out in 1981.

In the late fifties, the foot patrols were to a certain extent replaced by officers riding an almost silent, water-cooled Velocette motorcycle, known to the public as a Noddy Bike.

The police officers first had to pass a course in riding these machines at the Hendon Police school, and trainees would be seen on the roads around Wembley, following a normal police motorcyclist like a flock of ducklings following their mother to the farm pond.

Police drivers were required to be of a very high standard, and were sent on an intensive driving course at Hendon, which included high speed driving and skid-pan training. The highest attainment being a posting to the flying squad, an elite crime unit, as distinct from traffic patrol duties.

The police patrol cars were generally black Wolseley, six-cylinder saloon cars, and could be easily identified in the mirror by an alert driver, due to their having a distinctive chrome plated bell or gong mounted on the front bumper. In the forties and fifties, members of the public did not require ear protection from passing public service vehicles as is the case today. Some cars also carried an illuminated police sign on the front of the roof, and most carried a radio aerial mounted towards the rear of the roof area. Special traffic control cars also had a loudspeaker mounted on the roof to issue directions to motorists or the public at accident scenes. Unmarked cars on traffic duty did not appear until the mid to late fifties.

Due to the war, fitting two-way radio equipment in cars was delayed until 1946, when the network started up, using ex-military VHF equipment of the type used in fighter aircraft.

The same equipment was available as government surplus, and was used illegally by some members of the public for listening to the Metropolitan Police.

These early radio's took up a good deal of space in the boot of the police car, and used a great deal of power from the car battery. As the technology improved, and transistorized equipment appeared in the late fifties, the size of the equipment was drastically reduced and the efficiency greatly improved.

The motorcycle arm of the police generally rode on maroon painted Triumph 500cc Speed Twin machines. The uniform of the times consisted of leather gaiters with uniform blue trousers, similar to jodphurs, a standard police tunic, a peaked cap with goggles, and elbow length white gauntlets. It was said at the time that the first intimation of the arrival of one of these warriors, would be a goggled face looking at you through the drivers window, and a white arm waving you over to stop.

Generally there was very little serious criminal activity in Wembley. The occasional factory break-in or burglary, 'Drunk and disorderly', and 'Acting in a manner likely to cause a breach of the peace' were the most common offences. Any tramps or suspicious characters found in Wembley, were taken into custody, and at the police station they would be given a bath, a haircut, deloused if required, and examined by a doctor. Their clothes would be washed and next day they would be driven outside the bounds of Wembley and released. Begging in the street was also against the law, and this law was strictly enforced. Serious young offenders were sent to a Borstal Institution, or if old enough, given the choice of entering the army as a boy recruit, rather than to jail.

The other major public service in the Borough was the Fire & Ambulance service, based at Wembley Fire Station, a large modern facility built in the late thirties, serving as the borough fire and ambulance headquarters. Up to the sixties, one could find a red fire alarm on almost every major road intersection. The alarm was sent by breaking the glass window on the box, and pulling the lever. A fire engine would immediately be dispatched from the station. People causing false alarms if caught, were subject to a heavy fine or a possible prison term.

The new fire station, finished just in time for the war, was a modern two-storey building, flanked by two matching houses for senior fire officers. The main building had a centre entrance with glass folding doors on each side, each area enclosing a space for two fire engines. Above the engine house was the second floor containing crew rooms, offices, and sleeping quarters for night crews. A driveway on each side of the main building gave access to a large rear compound around which was further garage and storage space.

The entire compound was surrounded by a ten foot high brick wall. At the back of the compound was a brick practice tower about fifty feet high, with large open window spaces on each of three levels. The tower was used for ladder practice and for hanging up and drying canvas fire hoses. It was demolished later, possibly when a third storey was added to the main building.

Behind the fire station was Harley Close, a small road off Fairview Avenue, containing seven houses for senior firemen. Fairview Avenue led to Wembley Cottage Hospital.

At least up to the late sixties, the building was shared by the Ambulance service, with dedicated accident ambulances also on call twenty-four hours a day.

Behind the large glass doors in front of the fire station could be seen the gleaming brass-work of the big Dennis fire engines, each with a large hand operated brass bell.

The fire appliances were kept on the left hand side of the front door and the Ambulances on the right hand side.

The ambulance drivers in the fifties were given very extensive first aid training and worked in pairs. There was no radio fitted in the vehicles at that time, and the two ambulance men on duty had to cope with whatever emergency they found themselves dealing with. They had a good deal of autonomy, and would often have to make decisions which today would have to be referred to a doctor on two- way radio. This included the administration of Morphine to a seriously injured patient in pain.

One of the worst accidents recalled by Tonys' brother, an Ambulance driver, was the train crash at Harrow and Wealdstone in 1952 where piles of body parts were collected from the wreckage for possible identification by the coroner.

Boredom played a large part in the lives of the duty firemen and ambulance drivers at the fire station, and a good deal of horseplay took place during the evening and night shifts. This may have consisted of rolling loud fire crackers under the bunks of sleeping firemen around Guy-Fawks day, placing a 'Dirty Fido' plastic dog turd on the seat of the chief officers toilet, setting off stink bombs, and other harmless amusements. The day shift workers were kept busy cleaning and polishing the station and the appliances.

At the end of a long footpath through the St. Johns graveyard was the old town mortuary. When the ambulance men had occasion to deliver a corpse to the mortuary, the law required that a police officer be in attendance. The arrival of an ambulance outside the police station would therefore be the signal for all the officers on duty to disappear on various errands. The duty sergeant would then generally have to assign the newest and greenest police constable to accompany the ambulance men to the mortuary to undress the body.

The footpath through the graveyard was unlit, and the long walk in the dark, with a corpse on the stretcher was not popular even with the ambulance drivers.

On one occasion, on a dark foggy autumn evening, a fireman, having heard ahead of time that a delivery was to be made to the mortuary, hid behind a gravestone, and rose up with a groan as the stretcher was passing. One of the ambulance men, being of a superstitious nature dropped his end of the stretcher and took off back down the path at high speed, leaving the hysterically laughing fireman to help complete the delivery.

Every year the fire station would hold an open day. These were immensely popular with the public and would generally draw a large crowd. Children were allowed to climb up on the fire engines and ring the bell. The display would generally include dousing a large fire in the compound, a ladder rescue from the top window of the practice tower, hook ladder ascents from the ground to the top of the tower, and leaping from the top window into a canvas ring held by several firemen. The old tower has now gone, but one has to wonder whether the use of ladders by firemen, not to mention jumping out of the top window of the tower into a canvas sheet, would still be permitted by today's restrictive and some might say absurd, health and safety regulations. The age-old practice of sliding down a brass pole from the crew room to the fire engines has already been banned as too dangerous in many parts of America. It might well be argued that running down stairs from the crew room is equally hazardous.

Living next door to the fire station, Tony would hear the initial alarm bell, followed, never more than twenty seconds later by the fire engine accelerating past the house. A frequent customer of the fire service was the British Oxygen factory in North Wembley. Oxygen cylinders being refilled would frequently explode with a sound reminiscent of a bomb going off. There would be a boom in the distance, the alarm bell would immediately ring at the fire station, and a few moments later the fire engine would roar up Crawford Avenue on its errand.

The fire engines were generally bright red Dennis machines, the commercial division of Rolls Royce. The drivers compartment was open to the weather behind the windscreen, and the remaining firemen would sit or hold on at the back of the engine. (Oh the horror! Somebody might fall off.)

Up to the sixties, there were still a few of the old green NFS fire trucks left over from the war. These were generally looked after by the Civil Defence organizations or the Army.

The senior fire officers used Ford V8 Pilot staff cars, which were considered to be fast, but could be outpaced by the old 1937 Daimler Ambulances with the eight cylinder silent knight engines. There was a story circulating amongst the rank and file firemen, about a particular unpopular fire officer who was unable to keep up with such an Ambulance on Fryeant Way, with his new V8 staff car. He actually took the trouble to ascertain that the ambulance in question was in fact on an emergency rather than a routine call. These old LCC Daimlers were finally replaced by modern Bedford vehicles.

The traditional hand operated brass bell on the fire engines, and electric bell on police and ambulance vehicles, were used up to the sixties, at which time it was apparently thought necessary to introduce electronic noise-makers that can be heard at a distance of five miles, and exceed the threshold of pain for anybody less than two hundred feet from the source.

PUBLIC TRANSPORT.

Any more fares please? Hold very tight please! Please move down the bus
London Transport bus conductors patter.

Wembley enjoyed excellent transport services in the forties and fifties.

The Piccadilly Line stations at Alperton and Sudbury Town, the Northern and Metropolitan lines at Wembley Park, the Bakerloo and LMS lines at Wembley Central, plus the LNER steam services from Wembley Hill and Sudbury, all provided a fast and frequent service at fares that most people could afford.

At the time, all buses and underground trains were operated by the London Transport Executive, under the London Transport umbrella. The main LTE Facility was at Chiswick, but minor repairs and cleaning were undertaken by local bus garages such as Alperton, and trolley-bus depots such as Stonebridge Park.

There were at that time, numerous bus routes passing along Ealing Road and the High Road (Harrow Road).

The early post war period was a great time for young bus spotting enthusiasts. An eclectic variety of pre-war, wartime utility, plus the new RT types could be seen on the various routes. We also remember a few of the ancient outside staircase TD types being pressed into service to assist with the Olympic Games crowds in 1948.

In the normal course of events, most people would walk if the distance was two miles or less, and as a general rule, people at the time worked within a walking or cycling distance of their homes. For longer journeys, bus and train travel was the norm. Before 8 a.m. cheap workman's tickets were available on all bus routes.

Although there were telephone taxi services for the more affluent Wembley dwellers, taxis plying for hire were rarely seen, except possibly in the area of Wembley Stadium, having dropped off fares from Central London during a major sports event.

Among the bus routes serving Wembley as we remember them, the number 8B service ran from Alperton to Old Ford. Number 16, starting at Sudbury Town station, went to Victoria. The number 18 ran from Kings Cross and followed the High Road to Edgware via Harrow. The 46 ran from Alperton, up the Ealing Road, turning right into the High Road and up Park Lane terminating at Lambeth Bridge.

The 79 ran from Alperton up the Ealing Road, turning right into the High Road en route to Colindale.

The 79A also served the Perivale industrial estate. The 83 running from Ealing via Hendon to Golders Green also ran up the Ealing Road. The 83A followed more or less the same route, but went on to Brentford.

The number 92 ran from the Wembley Empire Pool and finished at Hanwell, via Harrow Road through Sudbury and along the Greenford Road. The 92A followed the same route, but included the Wembley industrial estate behind the Stadium.

The 662 Trolleybus, having turned at the Swan Circle, rests in the lay-by outside C & Q Stores, before starting its return journey to Paddington. (Mercury Motors can be seen on the left)   Below, Metroland postcard, courtesy of London Transport Museum

One rarely had to wait more than ten minutes for a bus, and with the aid of a bus map, or advice from the conductor, it was possible to travel anywhere in the Greater London area with relative ease.

Wembley was also served by the 662 trolleybus route, which ran the length of Harrow Road, from Sudbury to Paddington Green. It had been intended to extend the service along the Watford Road, to the junction of East Lane, but this plan was not implemented, and the trolleybuses turned at Sudbury roundabout. The trolleybus replaced the number 62 tram service, which operated on the same route up to 1936. The depot for cleaning and maintaining trams at Stonebridge was taken over by the new trolleybus service. The depot boasted a school for driver training, having in its confines a training circuit and a driving simulator.

The driver of a trolleybus, like a tram driver, required a special driving licence which was not valid for normal buses or road vehicles. The legal definition of a trolleybus by the Road Traffic Acts remained the same as a tram, and a group H driving licence which was in fact a tram driver's license continued to be issued.

This environmentally friendly, silent running electric vehicle drew its current from overhead wires by twin traction poles. Unlike the trams it replaced, which were running on tracks, it was able to steer around obstacles. It was a six-wheel vehicle, having two rear axles making for a comfortable ride.

Unlike the motor buses which had a half cab for the driver, these were full frontal. A bank of internal batteries, used for lighting and bell signals, also provided emergency traction for up to a quarter of a mile at maximum of four miles an hour in the event of a main power failure.

They had a seating capacity of 70, and were capable of astonishing acceleration, which could leave the unwary passenger hanging on to the grab rails for dear life, until the G forces fell to the point where he could take his seat. From the Harrow Tavern at Monks Park, down to the Wembley Triangle was a downhill run with only one request stop between. If nobody requested a stop, the speed reached by the time the bus arrived at the Wembley triangle might occasionally approach 50 m.p.h.. The trolleybuses were also popular with cyclists, pacing the bus, and using the suction created by the vehicle for assistance up hills, a practice frowned upon by the police.

They were clean, silent in operation, and less costly to maintain than diesel buses, although this may have been somewhat offset by the cost of maintaining the overheads. Another long forgotten feature of these buses, which was recently re-discovered by the manufacturers of modern electric cars, was the ability to regenerate electricity when the brakes were applied, thus saving energy.

Each bus carried a long bamboo pole with a hook, which was stored in a tube running the length of the vehicle. The traction poles were sprung to hold the trolley heads on the overhead wires and in the event that one or both became disconnected, the bus conductor if male would use the pole to replace them. Female bus conductors were not allowed to perform this task, so the driver would have to dismount. At the time it was considered to be a feat of strength beyond the capabilities of a mere woman. However, our recollection of some of the more hefty 'clippies', who were probably stronger than the less well-exercised drivers, casts doubt on this proposition.

As a result of the manifest incompetence of so called 'Planners', these excellent vehicles were all withdrawn from service by London Transport by May 1962, and replaced by the Routemaster Bus, widely touted at the time to be the transport wonder of the age.

With the passing of the trolleybuses, the Stonebridge depot was given over to fuelling and cleaning Routemaster buses, and the 662 service passed into history.

The Routemasters themselves were phased out after 40 years of service except for a few retained for sightseeing tours in central London. They were replaced by a series of off the shelf vehicles bought from various manufacturers. Previously all London buses had been purpose designed by LPTB for use in London and its suburbs, taking into account the areas unique problems.

After WW2, the 703 Green Line service was reinstated, running from Amersham in Bucks, to Wrotham in Kent. During the war, the Green Line services had been suspended and over a hundred of the single deck coaches were loaned to the U.S. Army and converted to 'Clubmobiles', equivalent to the British forces NAAFI wagons, dispensing coffee and donuts to the various U.S.

bases. Others were used as troop carriers. Green Line services were resumed as from 1946, and the 703s passed through Wembley on an hourly basis.

In the late 30s, construction had started on the Northern line Elstree extension, from Edgware, with a large train shed at its terminus at Bushey Heath. At the onset of war, work on the line was halted.

However, the shed had been more or less completed, and by 1941, was used for aircraft production, (including the four engine Halifax bombers) It wasn't until the early fifties that London Transport decided to abandon any future resumption of work on the project. It was decided to convert the train sheds to a bus overhaul works in anticipation of the huge expansion of its fleet due to its withdrawal of the trolleybuses. The works employed a very large labour force from the surrounding areas, many employees being bussed in from various pick-up points including Wembley. Alperton Garage would have a *Works, out of service* bus stabled overnight for early morning collection delivery and return of workers for the day and night shifts. When completed, the facility was named after the nearby village of Aldenham.

The train services at the time were also much used by the public. Wembley Central station was shared by the London Underground, Bakerloo line, and the LMS. Travellers to Watford or Euston would take the LMS train. These were normal sized non-corridor coaches, originally painted in brown livery.

Travellers from Wembley, wishing to use the Bakerloo underground line could take the LMS and change at Queens Park, or wait for the smaller London Transport tube train.

The Piccadilly line service via Alperton and Sudbury Town was exclusively London Transport tube stock, although after the service closed at night, with the current switched off, one might occasionally see a maintenance train drawn by a maroon painted steam locomotive, or a yellow painted battery loco.

The Wembley Park station offered a more diverse selection of rolling stock. Apart from the smaller Northern line tube trains, the larger London Transport rolling stock, used on the older Metropolitan and Circle lines could be seen as well as the big Metropolitan Vickers electric locomotives, pulling their very old wooden rolling stock as far as Rickmansworth, where they were un-coupled and re-coupled to steam locomotives for the un-electrified onward journey to Aylesbury. Tony recalls that the older London Transport coaches were provided with hangers for standing passengers. These consisted of banana sized dense wooden rods, covered with leather and suspended on a long tubular support by leather loop straps. Early in the war these were removed and replaced by the more familiar stirrup design. The originals were issued to commando and paratrooper forces for use as a cosh. Nothing was wasted during the war.

The LNER service from Wembley Hill station featured the old N2 steam tank engines. This service known affectionately to the public as *The old Push and Pull*, offered connections to Marylebone, or a day out in the country in leafy Buckinghamshire at High Wycombe or Princes Risborough. The LNER and the LMS, along with the SR and the GWR were nationalized as from first of January 1948.

These train services continued to run throughout the war, despite shortages of staff, women taking over many jobs which were previously the domain of men. The trains were noticeably dirtier than they are today, as were the station platforms.

During the black-out period of the war, tube trains running above ground were illuminated only by dim orange neon bulbs situated adjacent to the doors. Normal lighting was used in the underground areas. In the event of air raids, the electric trains would stop to avoid the frequent electrical sparking from the rail pick-ups, which could be seen for many miles. During wartime, the windows of many trains and buses were often covered by a glued-on gauze, to prevent the glass shattering as a result of blast. A small triangle of clear glass was left in the middle of the windows. Derek remembers trying to peel this covering off during his occasional tube train and bus journeys.

Those of us old enough to remember travelling on the underground during the war will recall the sight of families using the stations as air raid shelters. Tony spent the night in one such station, when having been taken by an aunt to London for a pantomime, missed the last direct train back to Wembley. Rather than wait for a connection at Queens Park station, which was covered by a glass canopy, the aunt decided to remain underground until the morning.

SHOPPING IN WEMBLEY.

Residents often make purchases out of the district, solely because they are not aware of the facilities afforded them by their local tradesmen. A perusal of these pages will show that their needs can be adequately be dealt with locally.

Wembley official guide. 1939

Wembley High Road was recognized as one of the premier shopping districts in north west London, and while there may not have been any large department stores in the town, the variety of shops and stores enabled the would be purchasers to find just about anything they may have been looking for. On Saturdays, shoppers would ride in on busses, from Harrow and Harlesden, and on the underground, from as far away as Watford and Kensal Green. Ironically, on weekends, Wembley residents would often travel in the opposite direction to sample the stores in these other areas for a change. The Sopers department store in Harrow was a popular destination.

Refrigerators were rare in the forties and fifties, and housewives would go shopping daily on foot, to get foodstuffs for the evening meal. Instead of the large one-stop establishments we have today, there were dozens of small stores, so it was always possible to find one close to home, be it grocers, green grocers, butchers, chemists, or ironmongers. It was customary to carry a wicker shopping basket on these daily sorties, and with wartime and post war rationing it was unlikely that they would be overfilled.

Some enterprising housewives would carry an empty cup in her basket, in the hope that the grocer might have a cracked egg available off the ration.

By act of Parliament shops were closed on Sundays, and for Wembley the afternoon on Wednesdays was half day closing time. The majority of shops closed at 5.30 p.m., and many also closed half day on Saturdays. Some family owned shops were allowed to sell certain listed items on Sundays. It was said at the time that this list was compiled in Bedlam. For instance it was permissible to sell perishable foodstuffs, but not non-perishable. Matches could be sold, but not firelighters. The list went on, and there were always the busybodies from The Lords Day Observance Society ready to report shopkeepers for these small transgressions. Ironically it was legal to buy the News Of The

World scandal sheet on Sunday, but not a bible.

About 75% or more of the shops were owner operated, and had been in business for many years and would probably still be in business today, were it not for the activities of certain unscrupulous banks. Most of the properties were leasehold, and in the normal course of events the lease could be re-negotiated when it expired. Sometime in the early sixties these banks found that they could sell the freehold of certain properties at well above the market price to outside purchasers, who would then refuse to renew the lease when it came due, forcing many long established businesses to close. This practice was outlawed by the government in the late sixties, but not before more than half the small shops in Ealing Road had been taken over and the whole character of the area had changed.

The shopping area in the forties would have included Wembley High Road, from St Johns Church, to the Triangle, and Ealing Road perhaps as far down as the Chequers Public House.

We therefore start our tour of the shops in the Ealing Road starting at Braemar Avenue.

On the corner is Wiles. stationery and art supplies shop. At the rear they had a print shop that specialized in copying blueprints, and the glare of ultraviolet Crookes lights could be seen through the side window of the premises. Next door to Wiles, was Sidneys tobacconist, followed by an undertakers, Greens tailors, a chemist, and on the corner of Bowrons Avenue was Dawsons furniture shop. Now we cross Bowrons Avenue. On the opposite corner we have the Express Dairy. Then comes a double fronted shop, Clarks, seed merchants, and supplier of pet foods and aquatic supplies. This store had a male assistant with a reputation for inviting young boys to accompany him to the pictures.

Within this parade we also find Saunders & Taylor, Radio & TV dealers, a combined ladies and gents hairdressers, Bunns sports and toys, later to become Peter Miles. A Garners 7X Bakery, an iron- mongers/hardware shop, Mikes café, Evans greengrocers, The Chocolate Box, and on the corner of Eagle Road, Boatfields grocers. The proprietor of this shop wore a very inexpensive and poorly made wig, which fascinated Derek whenever he visited the shop. We then cross Eagle Road, on the corner of which was Models, ladies fashions, followed by Bishops grocery and Goswell's newsagents and tobacconists. Then we have the toy shop, Hawkins Grocers and Bobby's Café, whose speciality was a hot cordial drink in a tall glass, popular with Alperton school pupils. Finally, there was a small industrial establishment.

There are now private houses until number 116, which was Wembley House, a private school for girls. A few more private houses, one of which contained a doctors surgery, Begg, Frazer and Taylor, finally bringing us to the balustrade where the Wembley Brook passes under the Ealing Road.

Next we have a block of 8 shops, one of which was a single-storey estate agents. This little parade included Columbia dyers and cleaners, yet another café, a government surplus radio shop, a bicycle shop, later to become in 1961 Maccari's music shop, a Mecca for aspiring guitarists. Another newsagent-tobacconist, and on the corner of Chaplin Road was the office of Osborne the builders, with a Gas light & Coke company workshop just around the corner.

Crossing Chaplin Road we come to Joe's news-agency, a greengrocers, and a bag-wash laundry. Then we have two half shops, one of which was a wool shop the other half, a threepenny lending library. This establishment, which closed in 1948 always had a smell of musty books and the fumes of a paraffin oil heater which the bookish lady proprietor used throughout the cold months. Then we had a butcher, next to an alleyway leading to Wembley Brook and the rear access to the shops.

After the alley, we find Cut & Quality grocers, an optician, Clifford & Clifford estate agents,

Gordons jewellers, Arthurs three level department store, then Demarco's ice cream parlour, the Home & Colonial grocery, Radcliffs chemist shop, which always had an interesting display of surgical appliances in the window. We then pass an alley with steps leading down to the brook, Robinsons corn seed and forage merchants, a greengrocers and Sainsburys, which at the time was still a family owned chain of stores, noted for cleanliness and good quality. An order of Butter or 'National Margarine' would be cut from a large block, and patted into a small block with wooden paddles before being wrapped. Bacon would be individually sliced to customers specifications from a large flitch hanging behind the marble counter. This was properly smoked bacon and did not spew white filth into the pan when cooked.

Leaving Sainsburys, we come to the British Restaurant, which later became the Labour Exchange on the corner of Ealing Road and Harrow Road.

This was where, young men having reached a certain age, would have to register for National Service, and be issued with a national registration number. Unemployed workers would go there looking for jobs, or to get their national insurance cards stamped. Continuing along Harrow Road, towards Sudbury, we would pass a Trustee Savings Bank, a shoe store, and a W.H. Smiths newsagents. Next we would pass a Dry Cleaners, and a Stationers, before coming to Halfords, which at the time was predominantly a bicycle and bicycle accessories store.

Next to Halfords was an old established ironmongers, Norlands, which dealt more with heavy plumbing accessories, Hot and cold water tanks, and such things as coke burning Ideal boilers, and Paraffin oil heaters.

The last shop before Ranleigh Road, was Williams Brothers grocery, a large double-fronted shop, with the door opening on to the corner of the building. This store, would issue the customers, stamped metal tokens to the value of their purchases. Regular customers could redeem these tokens at certain times in exchange for groceries or cash, based on a small percentage of their face value. For non-regular customers, the tokens would often end up as play money for children. It was also possible to return jam jars and certain soft drink bottles for a few coins, a useful source of pocket money for children.

Across Ranleigh Road stood the Wembley Police Station, approached by a short flight of steps to the front entrance on the corner of the building.

Beyond the police station there was a small parade of shops, including a motor showroom, a florists, a Red Cross depot, a tailors, Mrs. Mackensie's sweet and tobacconists shop, and Saville's Undertakers on the corner of Napier Road.

Across Napier Road was a large old house owned by Doctor Goddard, and his father before him, and a number of 1930's vintage bungalows and small houses, running up to Talbot Road.

Across Talbot Road, was a block of five Victorian three-storey houses, originally known as Acorn Villas, but later numbered 581 – 589 Harrow Road. Tony lived in 583, and in 589 was a sign advertising The American School of Dancing, principle Peggy Bennett, specialising in stage training in all branches. Many young girls in the area attended this school, but to our knowledge only one boy, John Ochner, a school friend at Alperton School. Peggy Bennett would often stage modest shows at St Johns hall opposite, where parents could come and view their daughters achievements.

After Acorn Villas, was the new Wembley Fire Station.

Beyond the fire station was the Fairview Club, a private gentlemen's social club, which more or less ended the High Road commercial area.

Across the Harrow Road from the Fairview Club was the Treggena Hotel. This was one of the few hotels in Wembley at the time, and catered for a more up market clientele than the Railway Hotel, which would be more popular for commercial travellers. The Welshman, Freddy Williams, twice world speedway champion, who rode for Wembley, was a regular customer at the Treggena.

Continuing back into Wembley, we come to a large private house with extensive grounds on the corner of Crawford Avenue, reputed to have been owned by relatives of Winston Churchill. Across Crawford Avenue, was a wooden board fence surrounding the vicarage, after which was the heavily ornamented lych gate of St Johns church with its clock, and the God's Acre church yard. The one time vicar of St Johns church was the Rev. Sylvester, father of the well known dance orchestra leader, Victor Sylvester, who at times featured at the Majestic ballroom in Wembley

The ornamental cast iron railing along the churchyard wall survived the war, unlike most of the other similar railings around the Wembley area, which were requisitioned for scrap.

At the end of the churchyard, before Thurlow Gardens were four small shops.

At different times these included an odds and ends shop a shoe repair shop, a second hand bookstore and a car hire establishment.

After Thurlow Gardens, there were a number of different small shops, including a Rediffusion TV rental store, an Army recruiting office, a sweetshop and tobacconists, Horne Bros, which supplied childrens clothing and school uniforms, finally bringing us up to Killips, a large department store, with premises on each side of Lancelot Road. The Killips store was dominated by a large square clock with three faces. The first half of the store dealt with drapery such as sheets and curtains, and on the other side such items as wool yarn for knitting, or making hook rugs, a popular pastime in the early forties, knitting and dressmaking patterns, embroidery silks and transfers, needles and many other such items.

One of the features of Killips, which was fascinating to a child, was the Pneumatic tubing device which would whisk away the money with a pop and a whoosh, and shortly afterwards deliver the change with an even louder pop as the little cylinder shot out of the pipe into its wire cage. These systems were not unusual in large stores in the forties, but Killips had the only one we remember in Wembley.

The Wembley market was situated behind the Killips store on the right hand side a little way down Lancelot Road. Walking down the slope from the High Street, beside Killips, one came to the art déco entrance to a public convenience, with steps leading down into the market. The main entrance to the market was a little further down the road. In the fifties, it was still a real market, with a greengrocer, a fishmonger and butcher shop. It tended to be frequented by the less affluent members of the community, because the prices were somewhat lower than the more fashionable stores in the high street, and the area could never lay claim to any prize for hygiene or general tidiness.

The smell of the fishmongers stall could be detected well before the entrance to the market, as could that of the public convenience, which lacked a full time attendant.

The floor around the greengrocer's stall contained the usual clutter of cabbage leaves and broken wooden boxes etc. This was generally cleaned up after the market closed.

In addition to those traders mentioned above, the market also offered a small café, a shoe shop, a haberdashery, a ladies' dress shop, a cosmetic shop, a hardware and kitchen utensil store, and a bakers shop.

There was also a small parade of shops in Lancelot road opposite the entrance to the market.

The entrances to these shops were raised somewhat above street level. In this parade could be found a cobblers shop, a newsagent and sweet shop, and the Hazel Press, printers and stationers.

At the Killips store, the Harrow Road becomes Wembley High Road, and the Ealing Road crosses the intersection to become Lancelot Road.

Originally this part of Wembley was at the same level as the railway when it was first built, but the whole area was raised by about twenty feet to match the level of the bridge above the expanded railway system. The Regal Cinema and Montrose Crescent would represent the original level. With shops on both sides of the road , even above the railway lines, a stranger to the area might not realize the railway was there at all. After the road level was raised, the High Road developed into the area we have today. The construction of the shopping centre of Wembley as we knew it, was more or less completed by 1920.

The shops from Ealing Road to the Triangle area comprised the main part of the Wembley Shopping area, with a large number of ladies dress and shoe shops, which the authors, being men cannot place precisely. In fact, there were so many stores, that it would take a stage memory act to reel them off in their exact order. We therefore content ourselves by naming the more notable establishments which we recollect, roughly in the positions they occupied.

Next to Killips on the left hand side of the High Road, there was a gas showroom, followed by two men's tailors, one of which was Burtons with its inevitable Snooker hall above the store and Blands, a ladies shop. Next there was Ward & D'arcy, estate agents, MMJ Radio and TV. At Toombs a gents barber shop with about 6 chairs, situated on a lower floor of one of the shops, with a short flight of stairs leading down from the High Road, a small boy could have his hair cut for sixpence. Next came Lyons Cake shop, with tea rooms above, a butcher's shop, Damants, Lovels sweet shop, and a bakery. We then pass a small alleyway with steps leading down to the side of the railway and to a mews area where the horses for the bakers home delivery service were stabled.

Past the steps we come to the Westminster Bank, and then the old town hall building, which with the completion of the new Wembley Town Hall, was used during the rationing period as a food office, issuing ration cards, and free bottles of concentrated orange juice and cod liver oil, for children. The old building was demolished in the late fifties to make way for a branch of the British Home Stores. We then come to St Johns Road. On the left hand side was the building of the old fire station, and a little beyond, the alley leading to the stables, mentioned earlier.

A little way down St Johns Road, on the right hand side, there used to be a long wooden single-storey building serving as a pet shop. Tony remembers going to this little shop to see the puppies, and kittens. On one occasion they had a chimpanzee. This little store vanished without a trace sometime in the late forties or early fifties.

On the High Road, having crossed St Johns Road, we come to a Barclays bank, and a large triple fronted Marks & Spencers store. Next we come to Wisemans, dealing in bath fittings followed by a Singer Sewing Machine store.

After Singers we come to Curry's, an interesting shop which sold a number of different lines, ranging from bicycles, radio and TV sets, small household appliances, down to torches and batteries. The notable thing about Curry's was the early form of hire purchase offered. The purchase was secured with a modest deposit, with repayment being required weekly, by cash over the counter.

Next to Curry's was an ice cream and milk bar, the second of the Italian run establishments licensed by the Wembley Council shortly after the end of the war.

We then come to Camera Craft, selling camera's, film and photographic processing accessories. Next door to this shop was Coopers, a ladies gown shop followed by the Wembley Music Salon, offering musical instruments and gramophones, as well as sheet music and gramophone records, after which, we come to the National Provincial Bank on the corner of Park Lane.

Around the corner in Park Lane there was an estate agents, an opticians, a dental surgery, and Park Lane infants and junior School.

Across Park Lane, was St Peters Methodist Church, long since torn down to make way for a block of offices known as Chesterfield house. After the church, there was a parade of more modern shops, with flats above. Amongst these was a gents tailors, a Derwent Radio rental agency, a florist, a milk bar, where Tony first tasted Coca Cola in the forties, a fish & chip shop, later to become the Paragon fish bar, another milk bar called The Cherry Tree, a tobacconists, Taxilux car hire, one of the earliest radio controlled taxi services, a car showroom run by Freddy Williams after his retirement from Speedway racing, and finally another, larger car showroom, which brings us to the old air raid shelter, and the beginning of the Triangle area described in its own chapter.

Across the High Road was the bomb site that was Wembley Hill School, later to become the site of Copland School, next to the Wembley Hall cinema. Walking back down towards Wembley Central, we find a large Perrings Furniture store, a variety of other small shops, including a quality confectioners, run by two old ladies, finally arriving at the General Post Office. In the alley down one side of this building one would see the red painted bicycles used by uniformed 'Telegraph Boys' to deliver telegrams.

On the other side of the GPO was another alley running beside the Odeon Cinema where children would line up for the Saturday Matinee performance. The cinema emergency exit opened on to this alley. It was possible to watch the construction of the new Wembley telephone exchange behind the GPO while waiting for the Odeon to open its doors for the Matinee.

Next to the Majestic was the up-market toy shop, mentioned in another chapter. From there we come to a number of ladies shops, finally arriving at Hodge & Parvin, another dealer in heavy plumbing equipment and coke stoves, next door to Woolworths.

At the time, Woolworths store consisted of a number of little island counter areas, each with its own cashier. Nothing was wrapped or sealed. The perfume from the soap counter was noticeable all over the store. Only small inexpensive items were sold. Originally everything sold would be for 3d. or 6d. More expensive items, for instance a hand drill in the tool counter, would be sold in pieces, and although the final price might be two shillings, none of the individual parts would cost more than 6d. This tradition ended with the shortages occasioned by the war, and was never renewed.

We then cross London Road, arriving at a men's outfitters which might have been the Fifty Shilling Tailors, a variety of other clothing and shoe shops up to the entrance to a little cobbled road leading down to the coal yard and sidings beside the railway station.

There used to be a little row of cottages beside the coal sidings. This whole area has apparently been redeveloped along with the railway station, and contains a large Sainsbury's supermarket among other things.

Then there was a tobacconist, which may have been Finlays, and the first entrance to the Wembley Station arcade, where a number of good quality men's and ladies' outfitters were to be found, including Dunn's hatters, Dorothy Perkins Lingerie, and possibly Lilley & Skinners shoe's.

The second entrance to the station arcade was normally the pitch of a newspaper vendor.

On Sunday mornings it was possible to obtain foreign newspapers, and American publications such as Saturday Evening Post, and a variety of 'Horror comics'

After the station entrance there was a wooden frame and weatherboard building alongside the steps leading down to Montrose Crescent.

The wooden building was used during the war by the WVS, and later by the TocH, until its redevelopment in the late sixties. The Toc H, a charitable organization dating to the first world war, identifiable by a dim lamp above its premises, would give rise to the expression that a person was as dim as a Toc H lamp

After the steps we come to Garners Bakery, Boots Chemists, Mac Fisheries, a chain fishmongers, and Salmons, a store dealing in light ironmongery, and a wide variety of household items such as candles, soap powder , etc.

Then there was a large double shoe shop, and finally another large fishmongers shop where kippers and haddock were smoked on the premises, often causing a choking fog of wood-smoke to blanket the pavement. At other times they would display barrels of pickled herrings, the sight of which was so reminiscent of vomit that it invariably turned Tony's stomach every time he passed the shop.

At the traffic lights, we arrive at the Railway Hotel, turning back down Ealing Road in the direction of Alperton for the final leg of our journey.

After passing the malodorous stairs leading to the underground Gents toilet of the Railway hotel, we pass the Eversheds off license, and a Confectioners shop, followed by Sybil & Norman, a ladies dress shop.

Then we come to a very narrow entrance like an alleyway, which was in fact a small timber yard, and could be easily missed by a stranger to the area.

The next shop was Listers, selling record players, radio's TV sets and gramophone records. This was the second of only two suppliers of recorded music in Wembley.

One of the salesmen would often invite young music enthusiasts round to his home to listen to his record collection, an invitation we always declined.

Next door to this establishment were the offices of the Wembley Observer.

We then come to W Sage an art supplies shop, which also did picture framing and a Jewellers shop. Simpsons American clothes shop is on the corner of Montrose Crescent. Just around the corner was Montrose Motors, a small garage with repair facilities. This little business had the distinction in the late forties of developing a method of welding broken car half-shafts, long considered to be impossible. This was very useful at a time when car spares were hard to find after the war.

In the alley way behind the garage was an Express Dairy depot. The alleyway continued along behind the High Road shops, to emerge at the bottom of the steps. Here we find the Yorkshire fish & chip shop, a funeral directors, a ladies hairdresser notable for the strong smell of rotten eggs from the chemicals used for 'Permanent Waves', and a corner paper store which also sold odds & ends and was open on Sunday mornings.

Back in Ealing Road we cross Montrose Crescent and arrive at the Regal Cinema. In the Regal Parade, attached to the cinema we find Bradshaws the opticians, and Radio Rentals. Continuing on we pass a detached United Dairies facility, before arriving at St Andrews Presbyterian Church on the corner of Union Road.

On the other side of Union Road is Coronet Parade, with a pleasant little restaurant, Coronet Galleries, dealing in second hand items, one step above being a junk shop, Vac Spares, selling vacuum cleaner parts and repairs.

Next there was the site of the proposed Coronet Theatre, which was never built, but was developed as a public library in the early fifties.

Continuing down the Ealing Road, past a number of large private houses and crossing Lyon Park Avenue, we then come to a little slip road, set back from the main road and shielded by bushes, with a row of smaller private houses dating to the thirties. These bring us to a small Methodist church, alongside the depot for Humphries removals yard, with the parked furniture vans and office. We then arrive at Frank's café, and an insurance brokers office, then crossing Douglas Avenue to a further parade of shops.

Beginning with a camera shop we come to an alleyway leading behind the shops.

After the alley there was a builders office, a sweet shop called 'The Hut', the Alperton Cycle Works and a fish & chip shop. Next to this was Sharvel's, a wet fishmongers shop. We then have Fruins, a double shop selling bicycles, and a men's barber shop and then Doris's Cafe. Finally there was a car showroom ending the parade. We cross Haynes Road, and pass the yard of Gildersleeves, another furniture removal company, which had its offices in Chaplin Road, then Clayton Avenue, after which was St. James Church hall, containing gymnastics equipment used by the Alperton school.

Before arriving at Stanley Avenue we cross a little road leading down to some small cottages, a relic of old Wembley.

A little way down Stanley Avenue, is Wembley County Grammar school, built on the site of the old Alperton Hall. Crossing Stanley Avenue brings us to St James Church, then the Chequers public house and the end of our tour of the Wembley shopping district.

WEMBLEY TRIANGLE.

> *You get some very odd people coming dahn there you know.*
>
> Dan the Lavatory man, Wembley triangle public convenience attendant.

At the intersection of the Harrow Road, Wembley High Road and Wembley Hill Road, once known as Wembley Green, there is a little triangular traffic island, which during the forties through to the sixties held gents' and ladies' underground public conveniences.

The surrounding shops and buildings formed a little close knit community, where all the long-term shopkeepers knew each other and would gather for a chat and a cup of tea at various times in their different premises.

The Triangle boundaries were roughly defined by Simpsons American car dealership on the Wembley High Road, Wembley Hill railway station in Wembley Hill Road, and the Greyhound public house on the Harrow Road side.

From time to time the shops on the parade would change hands, but the hard core of old timers remained.

We begin our 1950 tour of the area walking east along the High Road, passing the two timber yards, Winfields and Pendletons. This would bring us to Ecclestone Place, a small road running parallel to the high street, with the rear of the shops on one side, and a row of small very old cottages backing on to the railway cutting. The history of these cottages is unknown, but with front doors opening directly on to the street, they are typical of the sort of building erected in the 19th century for railway workers.

Ecclestone Place was named after a local builder, and ex boxer reputedly weighing 35 stone, nicknamed 'Jumbo'

Continuing down the High Road, there was a small used car dealership on an empty lot which might have been a bomb site, but no definite information is available. We then pass Snells bookshop and come to Wembley surgical appliances, known by the local teenage boys as the Durex or French Letter shop. It was presided over by a small poker faced individual, whose only clients seem to have been furtive looking men wearing raincoats, looking over their shoulders before entering, and leaving almost immediately without seeming to have purchased anything! The shop did provide a useful service to somewhat embarrassed teenage boys, at a time when Boots Chemists steadfastly refused to stock contraceptives, and the other chemist shops invariably had young women behind the counters. These red faced teenage boys added considerably to the sale of aspirins and other innocuous items until they were faced with a male assistant behind the counter.

The next shop was a ladies hairdressers, followed by a small petrol station and garage workshop. We then pass two more small shops, followed by a double-fronted chemist's shop, and then a double- fronted antique shop, the owner of which would park his black vintage Bentley sports car outside. This shop later became Wembley Photographic Supplies.

Next, turning up Wembley Hill Road, was a half shop, containing a ladies hairdressers and a workman's café, followed by Triangle Motors, an Austin and Morris car agency. Then we come to the Youth Employment Office, an estate agent, and a further restaurant.

We then arrive at the other end of Ecclestone Place, on the far side of which is a taxi office, and the railway bridge.

Crossing the Wembley Hill Road at this point we come to the shops of Neeld Parade, the first business being the Wembley News offices and printing works. Speedway supporters walking home on Thursday evenings, could see the presses through the windows, printing the local paper for Fridays edition. Next to the printers is a small newsagent and a ladies gown shop.

We then come to Wally Kilminster's double shop. Wally Kilminster was a

New Zealander, and a pre-war Speedway rider for the Wembley Lions team. The first of his two shops sold sports equipment and clothing. The second, a hobbies and model shop was more interesting. In addition to model aircraft kits, and engines, he was the Hornby and Meccano agent and always had a large impressive Meccano model working in the shop window. These were factory built exhibition models far beyond the aspirations of ordinary young boys, who could never hope to accumulate the number of parts required, even if they possessed the skill to construct such ambitious projects. However, the display had the desired effect of drawing potential customers like a magnet.

The next shops on the way around the triangle were a gentlemen's outfitter, a bakers shop, and a gents hairdressers, after which was a greengrocers, followed by the Victoria Wine Company off-license, suppliers of wines and spirits to the clergymen of the Catholic Church opposite. Finally we come to Phelps Publicity on the corner of Oakington Manor Drive.

Phelps Publicity, Signwriters, Poster and Showcard artists, silk screen printing and bill posting was a thriving business at the time.

1. January 1952, saw a nervous 15 year old Derek (no new years bank holiday in 1952), starting work as an apprentice sign writer. The proprietor Arthur Phelps, a truly unforgettable character, was a bullet-headed red faced, loud voiced, heavyset man with only one arm. A one time bill poster himself, he knew the business inside out.

Known affectionately behind his back as Wingy, he would conduct business in his office each morning until opening time, after which he could be found in the saloon bar of the adjacent Greyhound public house. Afternoons, he might be found in the Fairview Club, next to Wembley fire station, where with his one arm and a cue rest, he could hold his own or beat other members at snooker or billiards.

Some uncharitable persons might have suggested that the other players were intimidated into letting him win, but this is not likely to have been the case. He was a truly skilled player. Despite his affliction, he could drive any car, steering and changing gear with his one arm. Anybody unfortunate enough to find himself as a passenger would be given the task of changing gear. He would give the command "Up Three" or "Down Two" while he depressed the clutch - a nerve-wracking experience for a fifteen year old apprentice.

Behind the Phelps premises was the silk-screen shop, where large posters and displays were produced. The ink used in the silk screen process produced very strong fumes, rather like cellulose paint or glue. Ventilation in the area was poor and the printers were half intoxicated by these fumes. Arthur Phelps was required by law to provide a pint of milk to these workers to offset the effect. The young apprentices were more susceptible to the fumes than the older workers and sometimes had to be removed from the shop on the point of collapse. Arthur's response to this problem was to send them round the block a few times on the back of somebody's motorcycle, "to get some fresh air into their lungs". This lasted until he realized that the apprentices were using it as an excuse to get a ride on the motorbikes, at which time he made them walk around the same route.

Across the Oakington Manor Drive, we have the Greyhound Public House.

We then come to a small parade of perhaps a dozen shops set back from the road with a lay-by, in which trolleybuses would line up to collect the crowds from Wembley Stadium during major events. The first of these shops, being next to the Greyhound was an off- licence, then there was a second hand motorcycle showroom. Then we have Rusbro the tailors, two brothers who specialized in hand made suits and shirts. Derek used to have his band uniforms made at this shop. Next, a news agents/tobacconists, then an electrical appliances and spares shop, run by Cyril Spinks, upon his retirement as chief mechanic to the Wembley Lions Speedway. At the end of the parade there was a tyre supplier and fitters.

Crossing the High Road, we have a similar parade of shops with another lay-by, built post war on what used to be the site of a number of wooden huts housing Italian prisoners of war. The lay-by would also accommodate trolleybuses waiting to pick up the stadium crowds, and these would use the turning point at the triangle to join the line heading back to Paddington.

The shops with flats above contained among other things, the Atlas Building Society, a café, later to become Leslies Expresso Bar, a double-fronted builders merchants, British Building Supplies, and a greengrocers on the corner of

Chatsworth Avenue.

On the opposite corner of Chatsworth Avenue, one came to a Haberdashers and curtain material shop, run by an old couple. A very old lady dressed in Victorian black would sit in the back of the store wearing a beard! The shop was sold in 1963 to become the first Indian restaurant to open in Wembley. It was also the first to use the name "The New Asia". After years of bland tasting food many people including ourselves, quickly became addicted to this new culinary delight.

Moving west towards Wembley centre, we come to a Post Office, a wet fish shop, an Express Dairy, a bakers shop and an iron-mongers. Then we come to Barclays Bank, and the Catholic church. Past the church we come to Simpsons American Car Agency in its earliest form. The agency property was bisected by a public footpath leading to the LMS sports field. For many years a Donald Campbell Bluebird Speedboat was stored in this yard under canvas. This disappeared when the area was developed in later years, and the authors would dearly love to know what became of it.

The little island in the centre of the Triangle, containing the ladies' and gents' conveniences, also provided a turning point for trolleybuses during major sports events at the stadium. The full time attendants of the toilet facilities kept them spotlessly clean, with the brass and copper water pipes shining like gold and silver. Little is known of the female attendant, but the keeper of the gents' was another of the memorable characters of the area. Known to all as Dan, (the lavatory man) he would purchase his cleaning materials from the iron mongers, and over a cup of tea, would regale the staff with tales of the daily happenings, "dahn there" One of the services offered by his facility, was a 'Wash & Brush Up'. For sixpence, the customer would be given a small piece of soap, and the use of a clean towel and a clothes brush. Dan would bemoan the fact that the people using this service rarely left him the customary tip.

His weekly purchases from the iron mongers would consist of Brasso metal polish, Harpic toilet cleaner, and Jeyes Fluid, disinfectant. He would accept no substitutes for these products, and would return to his underground den, clutching his purchases, together with a receipt, and would not be seen for another week.

Another memorable character from the Wembley Triangle was an Irishman known only as Paddy. He worked as an odd job man and could often be seen in the area pushing an old fashioned builders hand cart, which he kept in his place of business, a large lock-up garage behind Neeld Parade. A good hearted soul, with a dry sense of humour, he was liked by all of his neighbours. He had a notable thirst for Guinness and would often be found taking an extended lunch in the public bar of the Greyhound. This gave rise to a certain degree of flatulence, one of his more notable but perhaps less desirable characteristics. From his appearance it was impossible to guess his age, which could have been anything from fifty to eighty years old.

Paddy often did small jobs for Phelps Publicity, which is how Derek came to know him. He usually had small items for sale, which in the main were of dubious provenance, and he would approach likely customers in a furtive manner before producing the goods from under his jacket. On one occasion he sold Derek an antique flintlock pistol, which he kept for many years.

The proprietor of the Ironmongers shop was another unforgettable individual, who is worthy of a chapter of his own in this little work. The business, named Nichols & Polge was a partnership, which his father took over on the death of Mr Polge. Mr. Nichols took over the business when his father passed away. Although perhaps not a member of the worshipful company of ironmongers, which would have required a full five year apprenticeship, Nick, as he was known to his friends ran the business successfully until his retirement in 1964. He had a rare sense of humour and was a true eccentric. He could often be seen standing outside his shop wearing a traditional brown warehouse coat, and a shoulder length wig made from plumbers yarn. He would exchange banter with his particular cronies who were passing by.

His eccentricity was a huge embarrassment to the resident plumber, Mr Essel who was rather straight-laced. Nick possessed an ancient open-top Jowet, two cylinder car which was used as a delivery vehicle for the business. On one occasion, he obtained a slightly damaged female window display torso from friends at Phelps Publicity. Having tied this to the radiator of his Jowet, wearing his warehouse coat and wig, with a top hat, he drove the mortified plumber to a job, together with a large water tank and a bundle of pipes, through Wembley High Street on a busy shopping day.

Once a year, with the help of sturdy friends, he would push the old Jowet up on its side, and paint the underside with heavy black bitumen paint. It finally failed its MOT test, and had to be retired, no doubt to the relief of Mr. Essel.

The inside of the shop was typical of a real old time ironmongers, with nests of small drawers from floor to ceiling behind the counter. These contained small items of hardware and each had a little label in a brass frame describing the contents. In one of the top drawers, Nick kept a supply of Durex contraceptives as a favour to particular customers. With his usual sense of humour, he had labelled this drawer "Tool Holders"

One busy Saturday, when his wife was helping in the shop, an Irish customer asked for a Rawlplug tool holder. Mrs. Nichols then took a step-ladder and reached down the little drawer without seeing its contents until she had placed it on the counter in front of the astonished customer. One can only speculate on what may have passed between Nick and his wife that evening.

Derek took up employment at the ironmongers in 1960 when Phelps Publicity suffered a slow down of business following the death of its owner, and made a number of workers redundant. He quickly learned not to be surprised at anything he found when he went to work in the morning. On one occasion there was a breast from a brassier display model in the middle of the shop floor with a chalk circle around it, and the words "Caution! Do not step on this". Behind the shop there was a yard with a small brick building serving as the plumbers workshop. During the fifties, on certain Wednesday afternoons, which were early closing days in Wembley, the workshop became the venue of a private cinema. The audience was strictly by invitation only, generally consisting of local shopkeepers of long standing, who would gather about once a month to watch 8mm format "Art" films, known as "Murkie Movies". These were thought to have been supplied by the camera shop opposite the ironmongers, which had certain connections in the business. People passing in the alley-way behind the shops would often be surprised by loud guffaws emanating from the plumbers workshop. Compared to the routine pornography one finds in newspapers and television programs these days, those short Murkies were laughable by comparison.

ALPERTON.

> *Alperton lies in the valley between Wembley Hill and Hangar Hill, and is now almost fully developed.*
>
> *Wembley guide 1939*

In Victorian times, Alperton was apparently a thoroughly unpleasant place in which to live.

Home to numerous brick and tile kilns, chemical works, a sewage farm, several pig farms, and a fish manure factory, the atmosphere must have been choking, to say the least.

By the time we arrived on the scene in the forties, none of this remained, and although there was relatively more industrial activity in Alperton than in other parts of the borough, the atmosphere was no worse than anywhere else in Wembley, the principal source of air pollution being from soft coal fireplaces in the vast number of new houses in the area, and of course the refuse incinerator in Alperton Lane.

Although the once efficient General Post Office could clearly define the boundary between Wembley and Alperton, we always found the boundary between Wembley proper, and Alperton somewhat vague. For practical purposes, Alperton might be said to start at the junction of Bowrons Avenue and the Ealing Road, extending east, up to The Fox & Goose pub in Hangar Lane, including the Carlyon Road and Mount Pleasant housing estates, south to the Perivale border where the Brent crosses the Western Avenue, including the area of the municipal refuse dump, and the Alperton council estates, and west to the Canal and up past cemetery in Bridgewater Road to the junction of Whitton Avenue East. This area contained a relatively large amount of light industry, interspersed with mixed council and private housing estates. It enabled the great majority of workers to either walk or cycle to work. Most people at the time preferred to find work close to where they lived, even though London Transport provided a long-forgotten, excellent and frequent bus service for modest fares up to the late fifties.

We start our journey through Alperton at the Chequers Public House in Ealing Road, opposite which, is a small parade of shops, starting at Barclays bank on the corner of Braemar Avenue. Throughout the fifties this bank had its delivery and collection of cash done by a London Transport double-decker bus, once a week, promptly at ten a.m. on Wednesdays. One can only speculate on the ratio of uneventful deliveries to armed robberies, were this practice continued today. Moving up from the bank, we have a tobacconist and sweet shop, Heather Bakeries, Batas shoe shop and Green & Barnes, dealing in radio, TV, electrical, and also Meccano products. We then find a half shop, which was a shoe repair shop, the other half selling wool and knitting products. Next was a small Tesco's grocery shop, where at certain times one could purchase a bag of broken biscuits for sixpence, then the double fronted motorcycle shop owned by Speedway riders Jeff & Wally Lloyd, emitting the evocative aroma of petrol oil and rubber. This was a magnet for a schoolboy, to possibly catch a glimpse of the brothers, and drool over the second hand motorcycles and speedway machines they offered. In the early fifties, they also dealt with rebuilt Austin 7 engines, and motor spares. This was also where we got our first glimpse of the fabulous HRD Vincent Black Shadow motorcycle with the giant six-inch speedometer reading up to 150 m.p.h.. This was a 1000cc V-twin, claimed to be the fastest standard production, road going vehicle in the world at that time.

Around this time, the business changed and became Jeff Lloyds motor spares, relinquishing one of the two shops, which then became a sub Post Office.

Finally, next to the school was a small workmen's café, described in an later chapter.

Returning to the left-hand side of the road we then pass the Alperton Baptist Church, presided over in the fifties by the Rev. Peck, with a clear view of Alperton Secondary Modern School across the street.

From there, a number of large older private houses on the left hand side of the road took us to the junction of Ealing Road and Mount Pleasant, where up to 1959, a stable or garage in the grounds of a large detached house contained boot and shoe repair business. Thereafter, this house and several others were demolished, and Glenmore Parade, consisting of shops with flats above was built on the site.

Across Mount Pleasant, on the corner of Sunleigh Road, was the Pleasant Café, a gents barber shop, Hive tobacconists and newsagents, an estate agents, and Walkers building and decorating supplies. Derek in the 60's worked here as manager when the business changed hands and became Marcourt Building Supplies.

Behind these shops, Sunleigh Road led past a few dwelling houses, to a small group of factories, the largest being Velvet Crepe Paper, which in the fifties and sixties produced toilet paper, but during the war produced cardboard products for the war office and 'Window', strips of aluminium foil, dropped by bombers over Germany to disrupt the German air defense radar. Derek's mother was an outworker for this company, cutting strips of foil to certain lengths, and tying them into bundles at home.

On the other side of the road, there were a number of more modern houses, dating to the thirties and a small cul-de-sac road, St James's Gardens, which connected to a footpath over One Tree Hill and the temporary clinic, improvised after the war from a gas decontamination centre.

Across the Ealing Road from Mount Pleasant, was a large parade of shops, the first two, being combined into a large Co-op grocery, and a chemist shop, where as a pupil at Alperton school, Tony was able to purchase a variety of chemicals without formality, including fuming nitric acid, the possession of which today would be enough to not only alarm the health and safety police, but also the security services.

Next was a shoe shop, followed by a combined wet fish, and fried fish and chip shop, a butcher, a greengrocer, and a bakery. Behind this parade of shops was the Co-op dairy milk depot.

A daily delivery of bottled milk for local distribution was made by a large articulated lorry, with a pre-war Scammel prime mover. The driver would reverse this cumbersome vehicle into the narrow driveway between the shops and the last of the dwelling houses, an act of remarkable driving skill. This same vehicle was still making deliveries as late as 1970.

At the other end of the parade of shops was an unpaved driveway leading to an area known as Kennedy's farm. A small building known as Pear Tree Cottage stood at the end of the drive, owned by a Mr. Bert Tucker, a scrap dealer and car breaker, whose' son Peter went on to make | a name for himself in stock car racing. In the forties and early fifties there was a row of derelict workers cottages between Kennedy's driveway and Alperton station entrance. All this area was finally cleared for the site of the new Alperton School, but as late as 1955, it was possible to look down from the platform of Alperton station on to the rusting remains of what had once been the car breakers yard. Tony's older brother recalled this collection of ancient cars being relocated from further down Hangar Lane in the mid thirties. With immovable vehicles loaded on to ancient lorries, and those with wheels either being driven or towed, the procession slowly made its way over the canal bridge to settle in its new location.

The Alperton refuse works opened in 1936 on an area of waste ground, which had once been a sewage farm. It seems likely that the evicted breakers yard had been located somewhere in this area of development. By the early fifties the whole Kennedy's farm site was suffering from advanced planners blight and was overgrown with weeds.

Kennedy's farm backed up to One Tree Hill park, and the rubbish choked remains of the old farm pond was still a viable spot for newt catching into the late forties.

.Returning to our walk down Ealing Road, we pass the Alperton Park Hotel, and a parade of very old shops, which included a greengrocers, a workers café, a butcher, Morgans general grocers, and a sweetshop and newsagents. After the shops, approximately opposite the entrance to Alperton station is the entrance to the Atcrafts works, which manufactured wooden nursery and garden furniture and general timber products. The site backed up to the canal where timber was delivered by a barge from Brentford.

Before they had a concrete wharf built, the timber was unloaded with a Coles mobile crane, until one day the canal bank collapsed, dumping the crane into the water, with its jib blocking the channel. It was some time before the wreckage could be cleared and barge traffic restored.

Between the Atcraft facility and the underground railway viaduct, were several old factories, including a chemical refining works, and a number of other small enterprises.

Alperton tube station was a fine example of the work of Charles Holden, replacing the original structure in 1934. In November 1955 an escalator originally taken from the Dome of Discovery at the Festival of Britain, was installed to take passengers up to the London bound platform level. Arriving passengers and those bound in the direction of Uxbridge had to use the stairs. This remained in use until September 1988. In keeping with the policy of neglect apparent in public services today, (2010), this escalator is no longer in service.

Outside the station there were three small shops built into the station facade. One of these was an estate agents, and another was a car hire office, later owned by Peter Tucker, the stock car racer, and son of Bert Tucker and the third being a Findlay's tobacconist.

Passing under the bridge we arrive at the Alperton Bus Garage on the right-hand side, taking us to the Bridgewater Road. On the left hand side is Rosemont Road, leading to several small businesses using the bricked-up arches of the railway viaduct.

One of the more notable of these was Stan, the Riley Man, a specialist in repairing and restoring beautiful pre-war Riley sports cars. Several others included small metalwork, and car repair shops.

There was also small terrace of workers' cottages, in a derelict condition, one of which was the place of business of a paper and rag salvage, and scrap metal dealer. Bundles of old newspapers could be sold for a few pence, and small boys would often be seen making their way there, pulling a home made cart, or pushing an old pram loaded with salvaged newspaper and cardboard. It was common practice for some boys to hide pieces of sheet lead from bomb sites in amongst the bundles of newspapers to bring the weight up. The presiding totter would never complain about this, as the lead was worth far more than the paper.

This little road was also the occasional site of a modest fun fair, with swing-boats, and stalls offering hoop-la, coco-nut shies, etc. and small roundabouts.

Today this space is taken up by a modern glass fronted building, now also in derelict condition, presumably to be in keeping with the old traditions of the area.

We now arrive at the junction where the Ealing Road turns left over the canal bridge, and the Bridgewater Road on the right takes us to Sudbury. On the other side of the intersection stands the Pleasure Boat public house, which is described elsewhere in this volume. It is worth noting however, that in the early days of the canal, a passenger boat service operated from these premises, taking people to and from London on a regular basis.

Behind the bus garage and along the Bridgewater Road, was another small group of light industrial premises including The Metal Box Company. There was also a newsagents, and Dowlings Dairy, a small family business.

Following Ealing Road east, we climb the slope to the canal bridge, passing the transformers of a small electricity substation, and a billboard. Crossing the bridge, we find footpaths on each side of the road leading down to the canal towpath. On the right hand side of the road, alongside the canal was the Key Glass Works. Behind this was the Glacier Engineering research building, also alongside the canal. The research building was the scene of a gas explosion in the early sixties, which blew a pair of steel doors opening on to the towpath across to the other side of the canal.

A small road provided access to these facilities, as well as the main Glacier Engineering factory which was next along the Ealing road. The industrial estate continues back as far as Manor Farm Road, adjacent to the council housing estate.

Opposite the main Glacier works on the left hand side of Ealing Road, stands the Plough public house, an old establishment mentioned in a later chapter, next to which was the Alperton Bottling Company, where in the early mornings, casual labourers were hired on a daily basis for loading and unloading lorries. We now come to Carlyon Road, leading to a housing estate intermixed with more light industry.

Crossing again to the right hand side of the road, we have the Lancia car works, followed by Dagenham Motors, a main Ford dealership, opposite Carlyon Road. We then come to Cromwell Court, a small block of flats set back a little by a service road, which terminated in Burns Road which itself leads to Cromwell Road and a small housing development behind Cromwell Court. There were then three small shops, one of which sold a lemonade type drink from a machine for one penny, and was popular with pupils returning from Alperton sports ground on a hot summer afternoon.

We would then come to the Royal William public house, a once lively establishment, long since torn down to make way for a characterless block of flats.

Next to the Royal William was Alperton lane, leading to the Alperton running track and sports fields, and the municipal incinerator and dump.

On the left hand side of the road opposite Cromwell Court, we have Vicars Bridge Close, and Riverside Gardens with small housing developments dating to the thirties. We then arrive at the River Brent, which passes under the road at a point where the Ealing Road, becomes Hangar Lane. From this point up to the North Circular Road we have Metroland type houses on the left hand side of the road. On the right hand side were two small factories, Arrow Electric Switches, and Wolf electric tools. We then arrive at the Fox & Goose public house, and the eastern border of Alperton.

SUDBURY.

Sudbury, otherwise Southbury, is that part of the district farthest from London on the Harrow Road.

Wembley official guide 1939.

With the growth of Wembley proper during the thirties, Sudbury declined in importance. For practical purposes Sudbury can be said to begin where the Bridgewater Road joins the Harrow Road. At this point there are also two smaller roads at the intersection, one being Station Approach, which terminates at the Sudbury Town tube station, and the other being Allendale Road, which leads to the Sudbury Arms public house and the Sudbury Odeon cinema. There is a small parade of shops in this area serving the Whitton Avenue estate.

In the fifties there was also a notable fish and chip shop in this parade.

During the war, the area of waste ground on the Wembley side of the Bridgewater Road intersection, up to the United Dairy stables, was given over to allotment gardens, and the sties of a wartime pig club, the location of which had been subject to considerable opposition from people living in the immediate area. It is not known if the target of 100 pigs a year was ever reached.

The intersection has since been altered, and turned into a large roundabout, a necessary measure to cope with the vastly increased volume of traffic along the Harrow Road.

There was also a large garage on this corner, subsequently taken over by Bob Keeler.

Continuing along the Harrow Road towards the LNER railway bridge, on the fields on the right hand side, part of Barham Park, there was a group of Army huts, later used by the Air Training Corps. This site now contains a private house. Opposite this house across the road, was a little coal office of wooden construction, associated with the coal yard at Sudbury and Harrow Hill station. The coal yard and sidings have long gone, and the little unpaved access road has become Roundtree Road, host to a collection of particularly ugly apartment buildings.

Later in the early sixties, a small Fina petrol station opened next to the coal office, and was notable for having the first machine in Wembley to dispense contraceptives, in the gents toilet, a facility greatly appreciated by the local youth.

Passing under the bridge, we come to Terry's Reception rooms on the left. For a short time during the war it was a British restaurant, and later, in the mid fifties this was the venue of a modern jazz club run for a time by Derek's sister and her boyfriend. Among the other shops in the parade was the Sudbury Cycle Stores, a Mecca for the serious cyclist. Here specialist machines could be built to order and difficult-to-find parts could be found.

Also in the parade was Keats, run by an elderly couple. The shop remained basically unchanged for years and sold odds and ends as well as sheet music and gramophone records. At the time the only other places in Wembley where records were sold was Lister's in Ealing Road, and the Wembley Music Salon in the High Road. In those days of the old Shellac 78 r.p.m. records, it was customary to listen to the record in the store before purchasing it. However, in Keats this didn't apply, because their means of playing it was an old wind up gramophone with a steel needle, which they seemingly never changed. The store was one of the few places where *The Melody Maker* music paper was sold, a weekly 'must' for any musician. This sorely missed publication was eventually overtaken in the nineties by the comic pop magazines.

Behind the shop in a one bedroom bed-sitter lived a tall thin sharp-featured man called Slim. We never learned his real name. On a couple of nights a week any youngster with a musical instrument was welcomed and encouraged to play and learn. He, being a multi-instrumental musician, was a capable teacher. After a time Derek improved his trumpet playing and learned a few major chords on guitar. It was at these sessions at Slims that he teamed up and became mates with drummer Carlo Little who lived in Sudbury.

Slim ran a small used car lot, called U.C. Slim, between the entry to Sudbury Place and the Kannibal Pot, which although Slim has long gone, remains as a used car lot to the present time. On the corner of this little entry were two half shops, one being the premises of Hares Photographers, specialising in weddings, the other being Frank Ryder, signwriter.

The Kannibal Pot (or the Pot as it was known) will be described in a later chapter. One incident worth recording was when Johnny Morgan, a very good friend of ours who had a permanent smile on his face, walked into the Pot one night and was set upon by a bunch of the regulars who took exception to his ear-to-ear grin. He was rescued by the proprietor who bundled him out of the back door, but not before he had sustained a black eye and a busted lip. Another Sudbury hooligan of the early fifties was teddy boy Mickey Murphy (name changed to protect the author if he reads this). This individual carried a bicycle chain as a weapon, and had done time in prison for GBH.

Derek and a friend were walking down Allendale Road one night after a visit to the Sudbury Odeon, each eating fish and chips from its customary newspaper wrapping. They were alarmed to see approaching them in the distance the dreaded Mickey Murphy.

With no escape route available, they stood aside to let him pass between them. As he passed, he raised his arms in a flash and sent the two fish suppers flying. They continued on their way thanking providence that Mickey had let them off so lightly.

Next to the Kannibal Pot was the Swan public house, which had a hall at the back that could be hired out for seven and sixpence an evening. Carlo and Derek used this hall for band practice. Realizing that Skiffle music would be the next craze, they abandoned their jazz band in 1956 and formed one of the first Skiffle groups in the area. Their first unpaid gig was played in The Swan. The mother of the banjo player, passing the hat around, raised the princely sum of seventeen shillings and eleven pence.

The excitement and enthusiasm for modern music was fuelled when Derek & Carlo went to see the film *The Blackboard Jungle* with Bill Haley's *Rock Around the Clock* as the title music.

Having been brought up on a diet of Vera Lynn, Billy Cotton and Frankie Lane, British teenagers embraced the excitement of Lonnie Donnegan, and the new sounds from America called Rock & Roll. While continuing with Skiffle for the months that followed, the group practiced and tried to capture the sounds of Chuck Berry, Little Richard, Carl Perkins and Jerry Lee Lewis, the giants of Rock & Roll. In the days before discos, there was no shortage of gigs for a group that was half way decent, so the boys got plenty of work playing at dances, clubs, weddings, and 21st birthday parties.

In 1958 Carlo Little was called up for national service, enlisting in the Royal Fusiliers corps of drums, very quickly becoming head drummer. Upon Carlo's demobilisation in 1960 Derek had moved on. Carlo met one night in the Pot, another local lad named David (Screaming Lord) Sutch and later formed a group that would become *The Savages*.

A couple of years later, while Carlo was playing with the Cyril Davies 'All-Stars', the newly formed Rolling Stones begged him to join them. He did in fact play a few gigs with them, but decided to stay with the All Stars. As a professional musician he needed to earn a living. He did however recommend Kingsbury drummer Charlie Watts, and the Stones went on to become one of the most famous Rock & Roll bands in the world. Sadly, Carlo's untimely death a few years ago closed the chapter on one of Britain's greatest Rock & Roll drummers.

Another local would-be drummer was 14 year old Keith Moon, who lived in the Chaplin Road estate, near Derek's home. He would be allowed on occasion to play with Derek's band on a couple of numbers at their Sunday night residency at the Victoria Hotel Rock & Roll Club in Rickmansworth. In 1960 these were his first appearances in public. At the time unfortunately, his playing left much to be desired since he just couldn't seem to keep time. Derek advised him to take tuition from someone like Carlo, which he did upon Carlo's release from the Army. The rest is history. Keith went on to become the drummer in *The Who* but died in 1978

Among the other musicians rehearsing at The Swan who became stars of the future, were guitarist Bernie Watson, bass player Rick Brown, pianist Nicky Hopkins and *Deep Purples'* bass player Nick Simper. All were local boys.

Across the Road from The Swan, was Mercury Motors, a car dealership owned by an Arthur Daley like character, who presided over a corner establishment at the junction of Rugby Avenue and Watford Road. Specialising in sports cars, their back yard was dominated by a pile of three-wheel Morgan cars piled on top of each other, any one of which would fetch a fortune today. On one occasion he had a rare Jaguar SS100 for sale, but for the most part he dealt in motors of uncertain provenance and mechanical condition.

It was however, the place to go if one required a set of wheels, and didn't have the wherewithal to put down the required deposit. Taking almost anything tradable in part exchange, they also had several motorcycles on display.

In 1955, Derek, being in the market for a motorcycle, was looking longingly at a machine on display outside the premises. "Like the look of it Son?" said the proprietor.

"Yes, but I ain't got the deposit" replied Derek. This was in the days when the law required a third of the total price as a deposit for any hire purchase agreement. In theory, this was to discourage people from buying products, which might otherwise be available for export. "Come into the office, we'll soon sort that out." said the salesman. "The bike is marked up for sixty pounds, right? If I put the price up to ninety pounds, I will owe you thirty quid, right? So that's your deposit. Sign here". The amount of sixty pounds was to be paid over a period of eighteen months.

Mercury Motors, was certainly the place to go, for the less affluent person who needed wheels, but the business suffered badly with the introduction of the MOT tests in the early sixties. Generally referred to as the ten year test, it was intended at the time, only for vehicles over ten years old, which more or less rendered his entire stock un-saleable. Many of the early Morgan three wheelers would have failed the MOT test even when brand new. Shortly after the introduction of the tests, a failed Austin 7 car could be had for as little as thirty shillings, and with the birth of the Mini in 1959 selling at just 500 pounds, almost overnight the roads became cleared of many of the colourful relics of yesteryear, and for about two years a meaningless blue MOT windscreen sticker was optimistically displayed by the owners of many old cars.

The building, originally named Mercury House, is now named Century House, and remains a car showroom.

The small garage next door to Mercury Motors has also survived, although it is no longer able to dispense petrol due to current regulations. The petrol pump was mounted on a pivot, which could be swung out over the pedestrians on to the road. This was a boon for the elderly, the infirm or invalids, as they didn't have to leave their vehicle and would be served by an attendant at a time when many garages were changing over to self-service.

Then came a short parade of shops including an estate agent, a tobacconist, the Mulberry Café, the premises of which would be hired out by private groups or clubs in the evenings. Finally there was another car showroom.

Continuing along the Watford Road towards Harrow, one comes to a driveway on the right, leading to the Vale Farm sports ground and open air swimming pool which was originally opened in 1932. After the closure of the Empire Pool, this became the only swimming pool in Wembley. At various times in the summer, groups of pupils were bussed in from local schools for swimming instruction. The sports field was home of the Wembley Wasps Rugby team, the members of which could be observed floundering about in the muddy field throughout the winter when the pool was closed.

After dark, the car park of the swimming pool, being relatively secluded, became a favourite place to park with a girlfriend and enjoy a necking session undisturbed by passers-by or police patrols.

The old open-air pool was demolished and replaced by a comprehensive sports centre, with two inside pools and a number of other facilities in 1979.

From Mercury Motors going towards Wembley, we have a parade of shops and a lay-by where the 662 trolleybus, having turned around at the little roundabout opposite the Swan Pub would wait to start their return journey to Paddington. In this parade of shops was a C & Q groceries, an electrical/radio/TV shop called Bruce & Buckle, a fish & chip shop, a baker and a confectioners, a half shop dealing with small electrical appliances, yet another estate agent, and a workmens' café.

This brings us again to the railway bridge, and the end of our walk.

Sudbury today remains a quiet backwater, relatively unchanged compared with Wembley High Road and the Ealing Road.

WARTIME

WAR COMES TO WEMBLEY.

I am speaking to you from the cabinet room of 10 Downing Street. This morning the British ambassador in Berlin handed the German government a final note stating that unless we heard from them by 11 o'clock that they were prepared at once to withdraw their troops from Poland, a state of war would exist between us. I have to tell you now that no such undertaking has been received and that consequently this country is at war with Germany.

Neville Chamberlain BBC 11.15am 3rd. Sept 1939

On the whole, Wembley did not take too bad a beating during WW2. Although most of the Luftwaffe activity was directed at the London docks, and the East End of the city, the borough of Wembley did receive its fair share.

War first came to Wembley one night in August 1940 when incendiary bombs were dropped on Barn Hill and Salmon Street, causing damage to houses in the area. The heaviest raid shortly after this came when over 1000 incendiary and high explosive bombs were dropped in the area of Lancelot Road. This raid totally destroyed the factories in the area, one of which was Goodmans Industries, manufacturing electronic components and transformers, and the company next door, which had previously produced gas fires, but had been turned over to the fabrication of aluminium alloy parts for aircraft, primarily Spitfires. The fire caused by the raid was so intense that the main water supply proved inadequate, and the National Fire Service had to lay 2 miles of hoses the length of Ealing Road in order to pump water up from the Canal at Alperton. Over sixty fire appliances were in attendance. The fire was finally brought under control in the morning. During this raid a few stray bombs also fell in Montrose Crescent, destroying several houses and damaging the Regal Cinema.

Derek recalls being taken outside by his father on the night of the raid to see the glow in the sky from the fires, which was so bright that one could easily read a newspaper. In retrospect it seems likely that the incendiary bombs had ignited the light alloy aircraft components, and such a fire cannot be subdued by water. In fact magnesium, a principal component of the light alloy material, will continue to burn even when completely submerged in water, so the firemen would be fighting a losing battle until the metal was finally consumed.

Derek went the next day to view the damage with some other boys, and remembers the area being covered with thousands of transformer core stampings.

There were many people who reported having seen a light on the roof of the Goodmans factory, and rumours of fifth column activity were rife. While these stories may seem far-fetched, it should be remembered that in the more affluent areas of Wembley, there were families living who had been great admirers of Hitler before the war, and some of them had been members of Sir Oswald Moseley's British Fascist League.

In total, 9000 bombs were dropped in the Borough including 526 high explosive, 7424 incendiary bombs, and six parachute mines. The first of these fell on 26th September, 1940 in District Road Sudbury, causing widespread damage. The site was subsequently visited by the King and Queen, no doubt to the appreciation of the local inhabitants.

There were also a couple of stray bombs dropped on the allotment gardens in what would later become Farm Avenue. Many people at the time assumed that the Germans were trying to hit the underground railway line. It seems more likely that the bombs were being jettisoned by an aircraft on its way home. If the visibility was good enough to see the Piccadilly line tracks, the airmen should also have been able to see many more attractive targets in the area, not least of which were the LMS marshalling yards between Wembley and Stonebridge Park, and the adjacent power station.

The air raid siren mounted on the roof of Wembley police station could be heard for miles, and during the early part of the war, sounded every night for weeks.

The black-out regulations were strictly enforced by air raid wardens who would patrol the streets looking for houses showing a chink of light around the black-out curtains. Black-out curtain material was available without the ration coupons required for clothing and other cloth items, and no excuse was accepted by the wardens.

The friendly invasion. Derek, his mum, younger brother and sister, have their photo taken by the girl next door's American Officer boyfriend, stationed at the USAAF fighter command HQ at Bushey Hall, Watford He took pictures of several families in the road. At this time, even if one owned a camera, film was unobtainable. Such was the generosity of U.S. servicemen stationed in this country during the war. Ever popular with the children for their gifts of gum, or a Hersheys chocolate bar.
The site of Bushey Hall exists to this day, and although the Americans left in the mid fifties, and the hall itself was demolished, some buildings still remain, and are now the home of the Lincolnsfield Center, with its 1940's house, military museum, blitz experience and victory garden. School groups visiting the center for the popular "Children at war" Experience, enjoy a three day stay, living and learning as evacuees in WW2. Derek works at the center along with others, sharing their childhood experiences and knowledge with today's children.

The black-out regulation also made after dark travel hazardous. Car headlights were masked off to a small slit, all roadside trees had white bands painted on them to increase visibility, and kerb-stones were painted white. Street shelters also had a broad white band painted around them. Walking into a lamppost in the pitch darkness was not unusual. Small torches became very popular, and were soon hard to find in the shops.

The anti aircraft battery beside Linthorpe Avenue, opposite Barham Park, would blaze away, more for the morale of the population than with the hope of hitting anything. Their activities however, did provide a wealth of shrapnel fragments for avid young collectors to pick up from the streets on their way to school. The shell fuse caps were particularly prized. School children in Wembley tended to look upon the war as something of a lark, not having the adult understanding of the dangers involved

In addition to high explosive and incendiary bombs, the Germans dropped hundreds of small anti-personnel devices known as Butterfly Bombs. They weighed a few pounds and after release from the bomber, the case would open and the bombs would flutter down making a soft landing. Many were fused to explode if moved, and like hand grenades could be fatal within an area of twenty feet. None of these were dropped on Wembley, but children were warned not to touch anything painted green, which resembled a large butterfly.

During the early part of the war, Tony's family would sleep in a Morrison shelter in the kitchen extension of their house on the Harrow Road next to Wembley fire station. This type of shelter was less common than the dugout or Anderson shelter, which could be found in many back yards at the time. The Morrison shelter resembled a large steel table with heavy wire mesh sides. It could not survive a direct hit, but if the house collapsed on top of it, the family could be rescued.

The Anderson shelters, although cold and damp, were much more robust, and we know of one example in Neasden Lane where a five hundred pound bomb exploded so close, that although the edge of the bomb crater was less than twenty feet from the shelter, the inhabitants emerged somewhat dazed, but otherwise unhurt. The buildings on each side of the shelter were very badly damaged by the blast. However, these shelters soon became unpopular. Being essentially holes in the ground, they were inclined to fill with water during heavy rainstorms, unless built on a slope with arrangements for drainage. The construction was simple, consisting of sheets of curved corrugated iron, forming an arch, which was then covered with the earth that had been excavated from the hole. Many people would grow vegetables on top of their shelters, as suggested by the Ministry of Food, and many had a wall of sandbags around the entrance door. Those who could afford it, might have a professional builder erect their shelter, with a concrete floor and brick walls front and back and proper ventilation, to minimize the smoke and fumes from the paraffin oil heaters many people used on cold winter nights. Council loans for the construction of private shelters were available, and advertisements for construction and types of shelters were placed in the Wembley News by local builders.

In addition to providing a shelter where appropriate, the government also provided every household with a stirrup pump, a galvanized bucket, and two bags of sand, to deal with the expected rain of incendiary bombs and the fires they started. Householders were warned not to throw water on an incendiary bomb, but to stifle it with sand. The stirrup pump and water were intended to douse secondary fires started by the bomb. From the children's standpoint, the stirrup pumps provided a lot of summertime fun in the garden, wearing swimming costumes and squirting each other. They were also very popular with amateur gardeners.

For those unfortunates not provided with a shelter, the cupboard under the stairs was a favourite refuge, and many people were rescued from these makeshift shelters after the house had collapsed due to a nearby bomb blast.

Later, a construction programme of brick and concrete street shelters was started in Wembley and eventually all the side streets had these shelters built every few hundred feet along their length. Some were provided with electric lights, and wooden bench seats,. Others provided with paraffin lamps, which were later secured to the wall with a lock and chain, after several had been stolen. In some parts of London, these street shelters had originally been built using mortar to bind the brickwork, but this type of construction lacked the strength to survive the blast effect of a nearby bomb. This was demonstrated by the destruction of such a shelter by a nearby bomb blast in Kenton. Fortunately it was unoccupied at the time. On occasions a high powered bomb exploding close to a shelter of this type would often suck out the walls of the shelter with the result that the nine inch thick concrete roof would fall on to the victims inside crushing them to death. The use of mortar was quickly discontinued in favour of cement.

Swinderby Road where Derek's family lived, had five surface street shelters, one of these being directly opposite their house. These shelters, during an air raid, would provide a good measure of protection against nearby bomb blasts, but would obviously not withstand a direct hit. However, they were not designed for comfort, and were a particularly unpleasant place to be if the air raid went on all night. A combination of body odour, (most people only bathed once a week, in the regulation five inches of bath water) and people smoking, together with the contribution from the latrine bucket, hidden behind a canvas screen in a corner, produced an atmosphere that was decidedly unpleasant. If this were not bad enough, the hard wooden seats, screaming children, and crying women, made sleep impossible, even after an exhausting twelve hour working day. Derek's family spent only one such night in a street shelter, deciding in future to take their chances at home under the stairs until they were issued with an Anderson shelter.

Derek remembers how, after an early morning raid word reached his street of a German parachutist landing in Ealing Road. An officer on leave two houses up from Derek grabbed his service revolver, and in pyjamas and dressing gown ran down to Ealing Road to find the police taking away a young aviator to the Wembley police station.

We never found out the circumstances of his landing or the whereabouts of his aircraft.

At the onset of hostilities, gas decontamination centres were also built around the area. These were very solidly constructed, and some survived long after the war. One of these was situated in Chalk Hill Road, and was converted into a dwelling house around 1954. Another was to be found at the back of One Tree Hill Park.

During the war, the entire area of One Tree Hill Park, and other areas of undeveloped waste ground, was given over to allotment gardens. All of the area now occupied by the Chaplin Road and Farm Avenue council estates was under cultivation, as well as certain railway embankments and other park areas. *Dig for Victory* posters were a common sight. Many people also kept chickens during the war. People who did so, had their ration of one egg per week stopped, but were allowed to keep any eggs their chickens produced. Tony's father kept a large flock of chickens up until the time that the hen house burned down due to a faulty paraffin oil heater. However, the next-door neighbour continued to keep chickens up to the mid fifties. The down side of home poultry farming was the inevitable infestation of rats, attracted by the chicken food. Some people also kept rabbits, which could be fed on garden weeds, but unlike the chickens did not produce eggs, and had to be killed, in order to be eaten.

Town dwellers were less inclined to do this and many rabbits survived the war as pets.

None the less, rabbit meat could be bought off ration at the butcher's shop, when it was available. However, it waned in popularity somewhat, when it was realized that a headless, skinned rabbit, hanging in the butchers shop with the feet removed, was indistinguishable from a headless skinned cat with its feet removed. Looking back it seems incredible that in the face of such draconian rationing, many people were still finicky about what they ate.

During the early part of the war, we started our education at Barham School, which was without air raid shelters. There was however, a corridor between the infants' classroom and the front entrance of the school. This was of heavy brick and concrete construction with no windows. When the air raid alert sounded the children would sit on the floor with their backs to the wall, and don gas masks until the 'all clear' sounded.

The smaller children were provided with a 'Mickey Mouse' gas mask a red rubber masks with two large round individual eye lenses, which vaguely resembled the Walt Disney character. These were quite popular with younger children, as when they exhaled it would produce a naughty noise through the nose flipper. Derek recalls his infant sister howling furiously when installed in her baby gasmask, which was an enclosed rubberised bag, with a large celluloid window, and equipped with a bellows to supply filtered air to its unfortunate occupant. This had to be operated by the mother or other family member. Gas warfare was thought to be a certainty and by 1939, every man woman and child had been issued with gas masks that were carried by the population at all times.

In the event gas was never used and people gradually stopped carrying them. This was just as well because the filters contained a mixture of asbestos and charcoal, subsequently discovered to be dangerously carcinogenic.

Opposite Wembley Hill School, (later rebuilt as Copland School in 1951), in Wembley High Road, a substantial buried shelter was constructed between the LNER Railway embankment and the road. Presumably it was intended to house all the pupils of the school, as well as any shoppers who were caught out by the raid. This shelter survived for many years after the war, and its dark corridors provided an interesting place to explore, for boys who could get their hands on a torch. One needed to tread carefully, as the old shelter was also used as a make shift latrine by people taken short in the High Street, or those who did not wish to part with the penny required to gain access to the WCs at the Triangle conveniences. The floor was littered with scraps of newspaper, and Richard the Thirds, giving the place the characteristic atmosphere of disused air raid shelters, which can still be experienced in those few remaining shelters and army pillboxes that survive around the country to this day.

Most of the children's fathers who were not in the armed forces, but were in reserved occupations, volunteered for fire watching and ARP work. Tony's father worked during the day at the London Transport works at Chiswick, and spent his evenings and most of the nights as a member of the St Johns Ambulance Brigade. Derek's father who was also in a reserved occupation was a member of the Home Guard. His rifle, an old Lee-Enfield, probably a relic of WW1, was kept in the front room of the house, and provided Derek with many hours of play, strictly against his father's orders. It was never known if his dad had been issued with any ammunition, but thankfully the old weapon never had to be used again in anger. With the crisis existing after the Dunkirk evacuation, small arms were in relatively short supply, and some Home Guard units were actually issued with single shot Martini-Henry rifles, which pre-dated the Boer war.

As in most towns in the country, savings groups were started and during nearly six years of war the saving public of Wembley amassed a total of thirteen million pounds, to meet specified objects, such as *Wings week*, *Weapons week*, *Buy a spitfire*, and *Salute the soldier week* for which 921,183 pounds was collected alone.

A coal shortage in February 1945, during a particularly cold winter saw emergency coal dumps set up at a number of locations, including Oakington Farm, Alperton Lane, Vale Farm, and St John's Road, where the authors dragged home the valuable fuel on home made trolley carts. Tony's recalls travelling with his mother on a trolleybus to the gas works at Kensal Rise, to get a large bag of coke.

The last hurrah of the bombing for Wembley was the destruction of the Wembley Hill School by a V1 flying bomb. Late in the evening the infernal machine flew low over Tony's house. A terrified Aunt was reassured by Mrs. Rock not to worry, "as it was probably one of ours". A few seconds later there was a tremendous explosion which shook the house.

The blast, which totally destroyed the school and an adjacent house, also blew off the roof of the Wembley Hall Cinema, putting it out of commission for some time. The loss of the cinema was probably considered a bigger disaster than the loss of the school by the population at large, because 'going to the pictures' was one of the few forms of entertainment available to the public other than 'the wireless', and was a great morale booster.

A total of 14 flying bombs fell in the borough before the war's end. The first fell in Station Approach Sudbury, on 19th June 1944. In total over five hundred houses were destroyed by the bombing and over eighteen thousand damaged to a lesser degree. Derek recalls his house having two windows being blown in and a plaster ceiling collapsing, this being typical of the damage caused by a nearby bomb.

Casualties numbered 150 killed, 402 seriously injured and 390 less seriously.

In May 1945 the war in Europe after six long years was over, and victory parties were held in many of the Borough's streets, halls and community centres, the largest being held at the Heather Park British Restaurant, and attended by over a thousand people. The surrender of Japan after the atom bombing of Hiroshima and Nagasaki in August 1945 was the occasion for more celebrations and street parties, though perhaps with not quite the same enthusiasm. A war-weary Wembley facing up to even more austerity came to realize that although the war was won, the good times might well be a long time in coming.

V.E. street party in Swinderby Road, May 1945. Redundant Morrison Shelters make useful tables, and Derek remembers the roof of a nearby Surface air raid shelter being used as a stage for band and entertainers.

RATIONING.

> *"Better Pot-Luck with Churchill today, than Humble Pie under Hitler tomorrow."* DON'T WASTE FOOD!
>
> Ministry of Food

It is often forgotten, that rationing of basic foodstuffs, and items of clothing continued in Britain for nine years after the end of the war. The housewife of these times had a difficult task shopping to prepare a meal for the family table. Although nobody ever went hungry, the daily menu would be bulked out with vegetables and bread, making for a very bland diet.

Vegetables and fish were never rationed other than by price and availability, as were meat products such as offal, rabbit meat, and poultry. Some items, which were available on a seasonal basis, or generally in short supply, would result in long queues at the shops that happened to have received stocks that day. Due to the wartime shortages, many housewives would automatically join a queue without knowing what it was for, on the chance of getting some rare item.

During the rationing period, it was necessary to register with a particular shop for meat and certain other commodities. As a regular customer, the housewife usually received more consideration than the odd walk-in stranger. This was particularly the case with un-rationed, but scarce items such as cigarettes or rationed items such as chocolate, which would be kept 'under the counter' for special customers. Derek's mother, a particularly good looking woman, was registered with Pierces Butchers in the Ealing Road. On occasion, she would have a few slices of corned beef or a couple of sausages, slipped into her shopping bag, with a knowing wink from the butcher.

The upside of the food rationing was that of a low fat, low sugar diet, making for a generally healthier population.

Clothing and woven goods were also rationed, with the exception of close woven black cloth for blackout curtains. This also had an upside, in that the average housewife learned to use her mother's sewing machine to repair or restyle old clothing. A very large percentage of the female population would carry a knitting bag, and at every spare moment could be seen knitting warm items of clothing, often using recycled yarn unravelled from old socks or sweaters. Make do and mend were the watchwords of the day, and nothing was wasted. During the war, hard to find condemned parachute silk was particularly prized as material for wedding dresses and underwear. Later in the war, the rare silk was replaced by American produced nylon parachutes. After the war, certain items of ex-army clothing could be purchased and modified for use as work clothes.

Even today it is possible to find old blankets bearing the distinctive double C label indicating that clothing points were required to buy them. Likewise the 'Utility' labels used on furniture made during the war are still sometimes seen on old pieces in salesrooms. There were a limited variety of items of furniture made during the war and these were generally well constructed, but of plain design, and inexpensive plywood and pine construction.

There follows a list of a typical weekly ration for the average individual. The list is not comprehensive, and many other items were subject to rationing. Each individual was issued with a ration book. These were of different colours for different categories of persons, for instance: General Adults; Children; Pregnant Women; Persons whose work required travel, and Merchant Seamen. Coupons were torn out of the ration books by the shopkeeper when items were purchased.

People living in hotels or billets, were required to hand over their ration books to the facility, but ration books were not required in restaurants, so people who were financially well off, were able to eat well throughout the war in expensive restaurants that were well supplied with black market foodstuffs. Although the government set a maximum price of five shillings for any meal, and this did in some measure limit profiteering by restaurant owners, it should be remembered that five shillings was a day's wages for many agricultural workers at the time.

WEEKLY FOOD RATIONS

Food item	First rationed.	De-rationed.
Bacon or Ham, 4 ounces	1940	1952
Sugar, 8 ounces	1940	1953
Tea, 2 ounces	1940	1952
Butter, 2 ounces	1940	1954
Cheese, 1 ounce	1941	1954
Margarine, 4 ounces	1940	1952
Cooking fat, 2 ounces	1940	1952
Eggs, 1	1941	1953
Meat, 1/10d (8 new pence)	1940	1954

(Meat was rationed by price. Cheaper cuts obviously going further.)

Potatoes and Bread	1946	1952
Petrol. Very limited.	1940	1950

Petrol supplies were very limited and it was supplied to essential services only throughout the war.

Pregnant and nursing mothers and children under five years old got first choice on oranges and bananas which made it through the U-boat blockade, as well as an extra pint of milk per day, and double the shell egg ration. Children under five were allocated half the meat ration, and those aged between five and sixteen were allowed tinned fruit, and an extra half pint of milk per day.

Each family was allowed one tin of dried milk each month, which would make four pints. However, a number of innovative recipes were contrived for making sweets and other treats using the dried milk powder. One of these was a rather pleasant peppermint toffee.

For vegetarian or religious reasons the meat ration could be exchanged for extra cheese. Heavy manual and agricultural workers were entitled to an extra ration of cheese.

Perhaps the worst felt shortage was the traditional cup of tea, which in 1940, was a mere two ounces a week. Saccharine was widely used as a sugar substitute in tea, but many people elected to drink it unsweetened rather than suffer the foul after-taste of the saccharine. Many people also took to drinking their tea without milk.

Families who elected to keep chickens throughout the war would have their egg ration stopped, but were allowed to keep as many eggs as their chickens produced. The number of laying hens was limited to ten per family, after which the surplus eggs from additional chickens were in theory supposed to be handed over to the Ministry of Food. How this rule could be implemented, and who was responsible for counting the number of hens is not known. However, since most domestic chickens were fed on minced up kitchen scraps, it is unlikely that the average family could support more than four or five at a time.

Powdered egg from the USA, in packets, each containing the equivalent of twelve shell eggs, became available with one packet issued per family each month. These would be used in baking cakes, although mixed with water and fried, it would also make a passable omelette.

Since it would clearly have been impractical to issue individual coupons for the wide variety of other controlled foods, these were rationed on a system of points, giving the public a greater variety based on individual choice. These points, worked on a system first introduced in 1941, started at 16 per month for a standard individual adult, but varied widely during the period of rationing to meet individual requirements and were adjusted to reflect changing availability of certain products for example

A tin of luncheon meat such as Spam,	16 points
Tin of sardines	16 points
Tinned fruit	8 points
Baked Beans	4 points
Condensed Milk	8 points
Cereals, (Oats, puffed wheat etc)	4 points
Rice, Sago, Tapioca.	2 points
Dried fruit	8 points
Biscuits	4 points

Derek's weekly sweet ration of choice, was a three-penny Mars bar, which he would carefully cut up into seven equal pieces, one for each day of the week. He would never get past two or three days before eating the lot.

In the late forties, a shipment of Locust Beans arrived from West Africa. They were un-rationed, and rather sweet, and while they lasted were quite popular with children. For a time, there were sweet tasting thin wooden sticks, also from Africa, which could be chewed.

A very welcome luxury for the sweet starved nation appeared on the market around 1950, when Penguin Bars and Wagon Wheels first appeared. These were chocolate-coated biscuits, and as they were classed as biscuits, which were off ration at that time, they were in great demand. It should be mentioned that all the above-mentioned treats, were a good deal larger in 1950 than they are today.

Some memorable abominations from the wartime period were the sawdust sausages, mentioned elsewhere in this book. (The Ministry of Food did eventually insist that they should have a minimum of thirty percent meat content. This left the consumer to ponder on the nature of the remaining seventy percent.)

Snoek, generally known as Snook, a particularly unpleasant type of tinned fish, was generally held by the public to be inedible. The huge stock of this commodity, purchased from South Africa by the Ministry of Food, probably went a long way to support the cat population of Britain at a time of food shortages. It became the butt of many a comedian's joke. Whale meat, became available later in the war, and although it resembled beef, tasted distinctly fishy and never became popular.

A constant grumble was the shortage of cigarettes and tobacco, smokers having to go from shop to shop and if lucky to end up with some obscure and evil smelling brand, probably Turkish.

The watering down of beer, and the near absence of spirits in the pubs that did manage to open for a few hours, was another cross for the working man to bear. Of course, for those who had the means and were in the know, more or less anything was available on the black market. As much as twenty pounds was charged for a bottle of whisky. 'Spivs' 'wideboys' or 'barrow boys', were always recognized by the trilby hat worn at a jaunty angle and wide shouldered camel hair coats or jackets, loud-patterned ties and a thin moustache. A perfect example would be Private Walker in *Dad's Army* television series.

They would on occasions be seen in the High Road or in the precinct of Wembley Central station, and often in the vicinity of Wembley Stadium during a sports event. They would stand with their open suitcases, glancing furtively over their shoulders looking out for the boys in blue. Derek received a metal toy gun for Christmas in 1944, which his dad bought from a spiv in Wembley High Road. The manufacture of metal toys was banned from 1941. The spiv sold a suitcase full of these toy guns in a matter of minutes.

The immediate post war period saw the height of the black marketers. Many of these men were deserters, or absent without leave, and at one time it was estimated that there were as many as twenty thousand British and American servicemen living on the run in London and its suburbs, making a living out of crime.

Clothing was rationed on the basis of each person being granted 66 points each year. The points were used as required. For instance:

Man's overcoat	16 points
Boy's overcoat	11 points
Gents trousers	8 points
Boy's trousers	6 points
Woman's coat, over 28 inches long	14 points
Girls coat	11 points
Woman's dress	7 points
Child's dress	5 points
Ladies stockings	2 points
Young girls stockings	1 point.

Shoes and footwear were also rationed, as was the leather required to resole them. In order to stretch the life of men's and boy's shoes, steel studs or 'Blakeys' were invariably employed, along with steel heels, resembling horseshoes, and steel toe pieces. Women's shoes were generally provided with rubber stick-on soles

Clothing was de-rationed in 1949, but food rationing lingered on for many years, the last items to be decontrolled being butter, cheese and meat in 1954.

End of Summer term Barham school 1948. Teacher Miss Prides class of 45 pupils would have been normal class size for the school at that time. Having sat their 11 plus, about a third of these children will go on to grammar schools in September

EDUCATION

BARHAM SCHOOL INFANTS & JUNIORS.

Stop, Look Right, Look left, Look Right again. If all is clear cross quickly but do not run!

N.E. Hill. Headmistress

Our earliest memories of Barham School begin when we were taken by our mothers at about the age of 5, and left in the infants section, a large and bright room on the left hand side of the building. This room contained small desks, innumerable toys, and a row of little mattresses for the children to take a nap after lunch. The Teacher was Miss Ames, and the newcomers were known as the baby class. Lessons began with learning the ABC, and adding up single numbers. Once 'adding up' had been mastered, children learned 'taking away' or subtraction. Also, chanting the two, three and four times multiplication tables began a process that ended in later classes with the twelve times table, and fixed in our young minds the ability to mentally do swift calculations. This appears magical to certain individuals of later generations who being educated by more modern progressive theories, were not taught multiplication tables by rote, and find themselves unable to add two and two without a pocket calculator. Learning to read by means of simple books starting with two and three letter words, working up to more advanced books did not seem to be a problem for most of the children, who could develop their reading skills at home by reading story books, without the modern distractions of television or video games.

The infants section was connected to the rest of the school by a long corridor, which also connected to a cloakroom, and the boys', and girls' toilets. The cloakroom was also used for the morning milk break. Each child would have a china cup without a handle, known as a beaker, and this would be filled with milk, ladled out of a United Dairies milk churn.

A short time after the war, the milk churn was replaced by individual small bottles of milk holding one third of a pint, given to the children with a wax-covered drinking straw. Derek's mother spent some time working as the milk lady at Barham School, as well as undertaking other war work at home while looking after her three children.

The corridor between the infant's classroom and the rest of the school, which was without windows, also served as a make-shift shelter during air raids. However, daytime air-raids were very rare by the time we started school, and the Luftwaffe wisely confined their activities to the hours of darkness.

There was however some minor damage to the girls' toilets, thought to be caused by a shell from the Anti Aircraft battery alongside Linthorpe road, which had failed to explode in the air and came down intact on to the roof of the single story building. Fortunately this happened at night when no children were present.

During the war, Chaplin Road ended about three houses past Norton Road, and an area of waste ground existed, bounded by the back of the houses on Danethorpe Road, and the wooden fence defining the Wembley Hospital boundary. This area was given over to allotment gardens, and there was a footpath running alongside the hospital fence, which connected to the end of Linthorpe Avenue and the side entrance to the school. From Linthorpe Avenue, Chaplin Road was again paved up to the point where it met the Harrow Road. Apart from a few bungalows, most of this area was undeveloped. This open land extended from the school fence to the London Transport railway embankment and as far as One Tree Hill Park in one direction, and as far as Fernwood Avenue and the Harrow Road on the other. There was a large pile of sand where Chaplin Road ended and the hospital fence began, which had originally been used to fill sandbags for air raid shelters, but was now abandoned and served as a favourite stopping place for games on the way home from school.

The head mistress at the time was Miss Hill. Although she was a kind and gentle lady, she was a feared figure to those sent to her for punishment, which normally consisted of slapping the back of the miscreants hand with her hand. It probably hurt her as much as the victim, but it was an effective deterrent. For very serious offences the punishment was handed out in front of the assembled school on the hall stage. Tony suffered the ignominy of being taken round to every class and punished for throwing stones. On this occasion, he was being pursued by a gang of bullies who had threatened to 'Bash Him Up.' The problem was that he was very good at throwing stones and came close to knocking an eye out of the leader of the gang.

Barham Infants & Junior schoool 2010.
The building still looking clean, modern and fit for purpose

Nobody was interested in hearing his side of the story, and the punishment was administered. In retrospect, a valuable lesson was learned by both parties. Tony learned not to expect justice in this world, and the gang leader learned to be careful of those whom he wanted to bash up.

Derek's punishment for running in the corridors was six slaps on one hand. When caught for the same offence two weeks later he received six slaps on both hands. Recidivist bad behaviour was not tolerated by Miss Hill.

Perhaps for this reason Derek has no happy memories of Barham School. He spent two years in Miss Flint's class, a teacher who had a formidable reputation for being strict, and terrified all the pupils. After retirement she took up private tutoring and displayed an entirely different, kindly disposition.

During the war, most of the teachers were women, and although it had been customary for teachers to give up their job when married, the war emergency brought many of these women back while the male teachers were called into the armed services. One of the few men remaining during the war years was Mr. Kettle.

Miss Hill referred to Barham as her country school, as indeed it was at the time surrounded on three sides by open fields, later to become the Farm Avenue and Chaplin Road council estates.

Miss Hill was also the author of the 'Kerb Drill' – for crossing the road. "Stop! Look Right, Look Left, and Look Right again. If all is clear, cross quickly, but do not run." This had to be learned by all pupils and was chanted at all assemblies in the hall. It was finally adopted throughout the country. From time to time the school would be visited by a police officer, who would talk to the children about road safety.

Mr Skinner the caretaker lived in a small house on the school property adjacent to Danethorpe Road. He presided over an enormous pile of coke, stacked against the wall of the corridor connecting the infant's section with the rest of the school. This coke fuelled the school central heating system, and climbing to the top of it was an irresistible temptation to young boys. These climbers were invariably caught by Mr Skinner, and taken to the office of the headmistress for judgment. Mr. Skinner's wife gave piano lessons in their little house.

During the war there were occasional distributions of very rare treats contributed by Commonwealth countries for the children. These included tins of cocoa, of a particularly sweet flavour, unlike the bitter English variety, sometimes oranges were distributed, and on one occasion, tins of jam from Australia.

An annual event was the visit of a photographer who would take individual pictures of all the children in the school. Derek still has a few of these pictures, which survived over the years. But due to a variety of domestic upheavals over the years, Tony's pictures were long ago lost.

Another annual event was the half-day holiday celebrating Empire Day. Members of the boy scouts and other youth organizations would wear their uniforms to school in the morning on this day, and everybody would get the afternoon off. Today, this celebration would be meaningless, because when Hong Kong reverted to China, Gibraltar, and a handful of tiny island dependencies spread around the world, are all that remain of the British Empire, now renamed the British Commonwealth.

The Colonial Office, underwent the first of several name changes and mergers, finally becoming part of the Foreign and Commonwealth office.

Research by C. Northcote Parkinson seems to suggest it is unlikely that the growth in the number of staff at these government departments would have been affected in any way, by this drastic dissolution of the Empire.

MEMORIES OF ALPERTON SCHOOL. 1948 – 1952.

Always cut on the waste side of the line lad – Follow?

Mr. Moray, woodwork master.

Having started our education at Barham School during the war years, our time there was interrupted by a short period of evacuation to the country. This was no doubt prompted by the destruction of Wembley Hill School by a flying bomb, at a time when it had seemed that the Blitz was more or less over. We returned to Barham, when the war was over, and were able to watch from the playing field, the construction of the council houses along Farm Avenue. One of these would be Derek's home for many years.

Having marginally failed to pass the Eleven Plus examination, we were delegated to be trained as factory fodder at Alperton School. Those who passed the exam, were sent to Wembley County School to be trained for work in administrative jobs in offices, or lower level civil service posts. At the time, the rigid class structure epitomized in the TV series *Dad's Army* was still well entrenched in England, and it was generally accepted that senior positions in government or management were reserved for those fortunate enough to have attended private schools and universities. The possibility of a pupil at Alperton School going on to a university was remote. The odds of being struck by a meteorite, we thought, were far better.

There could be no greater contrast, to the modern, bright, centrally heated classrooms of Barham School, than the Dickensian, gas lit, and poorly heated, Victorian edifice known as Alperton Secondary Modern School. A stranger to the area could be forgiven for mistaking it for a workhouse, and the architecture did indeed bear some resemblance to those institutions. One might almost have expected it to be presided over by a Beadle rather than a Headmaster. However, in the autumn of 1948, when we found ourselves standing in the cold drizzly playground, apprehensively waiting to be assigned to classrooms, such thoughts were far from our minds. School was something which had to be suffered, rather like a penance or a jail sentence, and no teacher in our experience had ever bothered to explain the advantages of a good education to the pupils in his or her charge, possibly failing to realize that what was self evident to an adult, might not be to a child.

During our stay at the school, some effort was made by Wembley Council to modernize the facility. The air raid shelters in the boys' playground were demolished in 1949 to make way for the Domestic Science classroom and the Metalwork shop. At the same time the main building was electrified and the old gas lights were removed. The improved illumination helped to reduce the gloomy aspect of the classrooms, but the air of sombre decay remained. The outside toilets in the playground were retained, to the relief of those boys who used them more for surreptitious smoking of forbidden cigarettes than for their intended purpose.

Being an old building, Alperton School was heated by large open coal fireplaces, each of which would consume as much coal in a day, as the average household would burn in a week. Anybody seated within range of the fireplace would be uncomfortably hot, while those farthest away would need warm clothes to avoid shivering. The school caretaker, Mr Priestly, who resided in a small house within the school compound, was kept busy all day, stoking these fireplaces from an enormous coal scuttle.

The heating of classrooms by open, coal-burning fireplaces continued throughout our stay at Alperton. The installation of central heating at that time would have been a major and disruptive undertaking, as well as being very expensive.

TEACHERS WE REMEMBER.

The teachers at Alperton were doing the best they could, at a time when the post-war socialist government was tinkering with the education system, levelling down where possible, and generally lowering the quality of education throughout the country.

With classes of 45 or more pupils they had problems enough without the need for directives passed down from the Orwellian bureau known as the Ministry of Education.

One of the more inane experiments was to teach French by a system of phonetics. The result of this experiment was the waste of a year's French study time for both the pupils and Mr Epton, who tried to convey the absurd concept of a flower pot in the mouth containing various vowels. The French language study was discontinued altogether by 1951. when the Ministry of Education apparently decided that factory workers did not need any knowledge of French. What little knowledge of the language we still retain, is probably due to the efforts of Mr. McAuliffe. His concentration on spoken French, and efforts to bring some interest into the subject with French gramophone records was far more effective than the experiments of faceless civil servants in the MoE.

Another experiment at the time was the introduction of Science as a subject. This could best be described as the orphan child of Physics and Chemistry with a few other odd subjects thrown into the mix. The essential relationship between mathematics and Physics was more or less lost, and from the standpoint of the student, a subscription to *Mechanix Illustrated* magazine would probably have been more useful. Being a subject that was neither fish nor fowl, it was worthless as a foundation for further education in any field.

The Science master, Mr. Jackson did the best he could to make the subject interesting, and formed a science club where members could build model turbines out of old golden syrup tins. Those who attended this club, learned to solder sheet tin, which can be counted as one of the few benefits of the class. The cosseting health and safety regulations would probably preclude the possibility of any such activity today. A student might possibly burn his finger with a soldering iron, or the syrup-tin boiler might blow its lid off and shower the watchers with hot water. This did in fact occasionally happen, to the delight and amusement of the club members.

The metalwork master, Mr. Trout presided over a well-equipped machine shop in a prefabricated concrete building, built against the fence on the right-hand side of the boys' playground. Mr. Trout taught us to use, make, and look after tools. These skills would be useful in the real world after school. Among the treasures in this little workshop, was a Myford ML7 lathe, a drill press, a small forge with a brazing torch, an electric hacksaw and a pedestal grindstone. The plethora of protective devices required today for such machines were unknown at the time, making Mr. Trout's life far less complicated, and his job of teaching far more effective than it might be today.

The woodwork shop was in the room projecting from the old building into the boys' playground. Having windows on two sides, it was one of the brighter classrooms in the old school. The woodwork master Mr. Moray was unquestionably a master cabinet maker, and was meticulous in his carpentry techniques. He kept a wood rasp in his classroom, which he held up as an example of how not to do things. When explaining anything to individual boys, he would end each sentence with - "Follow?" Another of his favourite pieces of advice was to always cut the wood on the waste side of the line.

All of the carpentry lessons used pine, the only type of wood available at the time. However, Mr. Moray kept a little hoard of rare hardwood, presumably from pre-war days, on a storage shelf above the entrance door to his classroom.

Mr. "Pop" Raisin took the class in technical drawing. He was a first class draftsman, who produced many of the sports certificates on display in the school corridors, and designed the school blazer badge, consisting of a tree growing on a hillside, emblematic of One Tree Hill.

He also had the ability to make technical drawing interesting, a gift sadly lacking in most of the other teachers, particularly those dealing with Mathematics. He was best remembered for the perpetual dew-drop on the end of his nose. He wore a battered trilby hat, and rode an old 28-inch-wheel bicycle to and from the school. He seemed to be impervious to the cold in wintertime, and lived in modest rooms in Bowrons Avenue. The technical drawing class was held in a poorly heated area towards the front of the school, which doubled as a dining room for the lunchtime 'Dinner'.

The Domestic Science class was situated next to the metalwork hut in an identical concrete building. Presided over by Miss Dawson, Domestic Science was apparently newspeak for cookery, and was only attended by the girls. It was rumoured that John Oschner, whose father was a chef, tried to get in without success. It is hard to assess the usefulness of the cookery classes. Most of the girls we dated in our spotty youth would have had a problem boiling a kettle without burning the water. Those who were good cooks invariably seem to have acquired the skill from their mother

The boys and girls had separate PT instruction. The girls would normally play netball on the courts behind the school. The girls PT instructor, Miss Richie, was a well endowed young woman, and the sight of her jumping around on the netball court in shorts and a tight sweater, could have a very unsettling effect on any boy who managed to sneak around to the area when she was taking a class. It was whispered that she had a similar effect on several members of the male staff.

The boys PT instructor liked to think he was applying army style training And any boy who for whatever reason was not a member of a sports team, or a star of the running track, was sent out on a 'cross country run' wearing only shorts and vest, regardless of the weather conditions at the time. While the class was out on the run, he would retire to the staff room and drink tea, while pursuing the attentions of some of the younger female teachers.

The course of this run was always the same. Down Ealing Road to the bus garage, up the length of Bridgewater Road into Fernwood Avenue and Chaplin Road, through Farm Avenue and back to the school via One Tree Hill Park. As part of his 'toughening-up' policy, it was his custom to ignore or tear up sick notes presented by boys who for one reason or another had been away from school for illness. One such boy was recovering from pneumonia, and happened to live in Farm Avenue. As he passed his house, his father was working in the front garden. The boy was sent indoors, and the father followed the remainder of the runners to the school. The altercation that followed in Mr. Hostler's office, was rumoured to have resulted in a bloody nose for the PT instructor, and threats of legal action by both parties.

The toughening-up policy ended abruptly.

There was also a diminutive Japanese exchange teacher specialising in gymnastics who came to the school for a short time around 1950. His real name is long-forgotten, but he was known as "Who Flung Dung" to the boys. The gymnastics class was generally held in St James Church Hall in Ealing Road. This building was heated in winter by a coke-burning stove, which was inclined to leak carbon monoxide fumes into the room, causing coughing attacks and headaches amongst the boys. The hall contained a vaulting horse and parallel bars, together with a variety of other exercise aids, not available in the main school buildings.

Mr. MacDonald took the music class during our first year at the school. This was before electrification. One late afternoon, when it became dark and gloomy in the hall, he found himself without matches to light the gas lamps. He asked if any of the class had matches, and one boy produced a box. Having lit the gas lamps, he ordered the boy to report to him after class to discuss his possession of forbidden matches and be awarded punishment for the offence.

Other music teachers included Miss Wraith who also taught art, and drove a pre-war Ford Anglia car. Cars were fairly rare in those days, particularly for somebody drawing a teacher's salary. The only other teachers' car was a very old Austin 7, owned by Mr Ferguson.

Mr Jackson, the science master rode a converted bicycle with a clip-on engine, sold commercially as *The Minimotor* fixed over the rear wheel on a special carrier. By way of contrast, the headmaster, Mr Timothy Hostler, would arrive each day on a bus.

Mr Popay, who took the fourth year boys class, was a pipe smoker, which he lit with an old petrol lighter that leaked into his pockets. He was invariably accompanied by a cloud of Ronson lighter fluid vapour, which could be detected from the back of the classroom by anybody with a normal sense of smell. Today, such an accumulation of fumes would probably result in the evacuation of the school, while Hazmat teams with breathing apparatus conducted a search for the cause.

Miss Harbour was a young woman who was past the first bloom of youth, and having probably lost her fiancée in the war, found herself 'on the shelf'. It was rumoured that she had an affair with one of the teachers, who then turned his attentions to the younger more nubile staff, causing her a great deal of unhappiness.

Mr Epton took the upper stream boys & girls for French and general subjects. He had some sort of arrangement with Gibbs Toothpaste where the pupils were given a form to tick off each day confirming that they had brushed their teeth. It is not known whether there was a financial consideration. He was a virulent anti-communist and on one occasion made the observation that; "The classroom door could suddenly fly open, and a communist with a machine-gun could kill you all in an instant". The absurdity of this remark was not lost on many of the pupils from the Alperton Estate, whose parents were sympathizers, if not card holding members of the communist party.

The headmaster, 'Tim' Hostler was a remote figure in his office at the front of the school. He would make an appearance at the assemblies in the main hall, and administer the occasional public caning for particularly heinous offences. It was rumoured that he had a wooden leg, and he did indeed walk with a limp.

THE DINNER QUEUE.

At mid-day, the pupils were required to line up in the playground for the school 'Dinner'. The covered corridor joining the two halves of the old school separated the girls' playground from the boys', with the girls on the Alperton side. A teacher was detailed to supervise the queue on the boys' side, which was usually a chaotic scene of shouting and pushing, with the supervising teacher either through inability or lack of interest, totally failing to maintain order. The main troublemakers were a group of thugs, for want of a better word, who terrorized fellow pupils and most teachers alike. However, since they were, for the most part, the star players in the school sports teams they were tolerated at the expense of the majority. One day, Mr Dung, the Japanese exchange teacher, took his turn as supervisor of the boys queue for the first time. Blowing his whistle, he shouted "shut up" in a loud voice. There was a pause in the pushing and shoving and a moment of quiet, broken by the sniggers of the usual troublemakers.

The little Japanese walked up to the biggest member of the group and gave him a backhand slap on the face, which laid him full length on the playground. "I said shut up" he shouted. After this you could have heard a pin drop. There was some talk among the gang about 'bashing him up' after school, but when it became known that he was a Ju-Jitsu expert the matter was quickly forgotten.

That little teacher was worthy of admiration. With the war just ended, and Japanese atrocity stories still being told, it took a great deal of courage to become an exchange teacher in England. His performance at the dinner queue was greatly appreciated by the majority of boys, and it is a pity that more of the teachers failed to share his intolerance for unruly behaviour.

THE SCHOOL NURSE.

From the standpoint of the pupils, one of the least agreeable events was the visit of the school nurse to check them for a variety of possible ailments, including head lice. Once a year she would arrive accompanied by a doctor, and the third year boys would have to line up to be called in one at a time to drop their trousers, cough, and have their testicles examined. As if having their Albert Halls handled by the Doctor was not bad enough, the presence of the nurse during these examinations was a further cause of embarrassment to the boys, particularly those who suffered an involuntary erection during the procedure.

The nurse, being a mature lady who had seen it all before, would administer a sharp tap with her pencil which it was said, caused immediate deflation of the offending organ.

Perhaps even less popular, was the visit of the school dentist who would hand out notes to attend the clinic located in One Tree Hill Park, behind St James's Gardens. During one of these visits Tony was given a note to have thirteen fillings.

Being at the time terrified of the Dentist, he tore up the note and threw it away. He spent the next six months worrying about the possible consequences of this, but there was no follow-up, and in time forgot the matter. Ten years later, while serving in the RAF, he was told by the medical officer that he was the only person on the camp with a full set of healthy teeth. Now in his 70s, he still has most of his teeth, but there is no doubt that if he had attended the clinic at the appointed time, he would have been wearing dentures years ago. What the National Health Service dentists at the time may have lacked in skill, they made up for in enthusiasm. It might even be suspected that they were paid at a piece rate for fillings. The health service was new at the time, and it was said to be Labour Party dogma, that everybody in England should have free eye glasses and false teeth, whether they needed them or not.

Another Government program of the time, was the eradication of TB in the UK. This ambitious scheme was run by the Medical Research Council, and every child in the country was given a scratch test to determine if he or she had been exposed to the disease. Those who showed no reaction to the scratch test were given a further injection which was in effect, a mild case of TB to enable their bodies to develop a resistance to the affliction.

The project would no doubt have succeeded in ridding the country of this disease, were it not for the later flood of third world immigrants in the fifties and sixties, who brought not only TB, but Smallpox with them. Today, although Smallpox has supposedly been eradicated, TB is alive and well in the UK and apparently resistant to many of the antibiotics which might once have virtually eliminated it.

MURDER MOST FOUL.

In 1950 the school won the distinction of having one of its boys arrested for murder. The boy in question was accused of deliberately drowning a younger boy in the river Brent behind the Alperton municipal dump. The case enjoyed the full attention of the *News of the World* and the *Daily Mirror* while it lasted. The boy was found guilty, but being a minor, was not sentenced to 'The Drop' as would have been the case with an adult. He was ordered to be detained, 'At Her Majesties Pleasure', and was never heard of at the school again.

SCHOOL SPORTS.

The winter weather did nothing to dampen the enthusiasm of the sports fanatics, and once a week we would find ourselves marched or driven by chartered coach, down to the Alperton sports field, to kick a ball around in the mud, generally in a misty drizzle.

The sports field was situated in Alperton Lane, opposite the Alperton dump. This facility was still producing pig feed, by cooking up waste food collected in special bins on street corners all around Wembley. The product was well regarded by farmers, but less so by the residents who lived close to the foul smelling collection bins, suffering the flies and stench they produced throughout the summer months. The end product of this wartime measure was known as 'Wembley Pudding', and was cooked up on Wednesdays, the chosen day for sports by the school. The smell from the cooking process would permeate the entire area, including the football fields and running track, combining with the normal winter smog and industrial air pollution to provide a thoroughly unhealthy environment.

These unwelcome episodes instilled in us a lifelong horror of any pastime involving balls, running around in circles, or sports generally.

During the summer months swimming was offered as an alternative to cricket, or running around in circles on the track. This was available at the Vale Farm swimming baths in Sudbury. It could have been a productive and enjoyable change were it not for the total lack of control exercised by the attendant teachers. The usual hooligans were allowed to run amok, pushing other people into the pool, and it is a mystery, that some of the non-swimmers were not drowned. Fortunately it was possible to opt out of swimming and indulge in quiet study in the otherwise deserted classroom.

In order to foster a spirit of competition, the school population was split into four groups, or 'Houses', these being York, Tudor, Lancaster, and Stuart. Each 'House' was given a representative colour. The whole concept was presumably based on the Wars of the Roses, and subsequent dynastic struggles, and was enthusiastically embraced by the majority of sports fans. To the sport-hating minority, it was just another pointless and boring waste of time.

SCHOOL DINNERS.

For those pupils unable to get home during the lunch break, hot meals were available at the school for a few pence. The meals were filling, and the menu was probably compiled by government nutritionists who did not have to partake of it themselves. Boiled cabbage and reconstituted powdered potato, served with grey, watery minced beef, was a regular feature of the bill of fare, followed by a desert which may have been steamed pudding with watery custard poured over it, or tapioca, a glutinous mess resembling frog spawn.

To be fair, the food was probably no worse than that served in HM prisons, or the Army, and was likely better than that which some of the pupils would get at home.

During 1948, food rationing was still fully in effect, and actually worse than during the war years with bread and potatoes being included for the first time.

The venue for these lunchtime meals, doubled as the technical drawing classroom, and the smell of boiled cabbage would linger for the rest of the afternoon, adding to the general institutional atmosphere of the school.

PLAYGROUND ACTIVITIES.

In the morning, before classes, during the lunch time break, and mid afternoon 'Playtime' a variety of activities commonly took place in the boys' playground, ranging from rough and sometimes dangerous games, bullying by gangs of thugs, smoking in the toilets, and trading for cigarette cards, which, although they had not been included in packets of cigarettes since the start of WW2, seemed to be available by the thousand, and formed a useful secondary currency. Real money was not plentiful at the time. Second to cigarette cards were glass marbles, which varied in value, based on size and colour. The third main commodity was of course individual cigarettes and matches. The least expensive of these at the time were 'Weights' and 'Woodbines', both available in packets of five, or as individual cigarettes from certain tobacconists. Since cash was required to purchase these, they tended to become the gold standard against which all other playground commodities were measured.

There was also a thriving trade in pre-war Dinky Toys. These popular die-cast models had just become available again in very limited quantities. The pre-war models might be regarded as the antique objects d'art of the playground economy.

One of the games played with cigarette cards was for a boy to lay a card down on the playground, generally close to a wall. Other boys would then stand back an agreed distance, normally about six feet, and try to flick their own cards to land on top of the 'target' card. Failure to do this would result in the loss of the challenger's card. A lucky winner would claim all the cards on the ground. This playground game was regarded as gambling by Tim, and occasional efforts were made to stop it. However, it could be argued that it was clearly a 'Game of Skill', not covered by the gambling laws.

One of the more popular, inexpensive toys available at the time was a model bomb, consisting of two parts tied together with string. Paper caps, of the type used in toy pistols were inserted between the two halves of the bomb, and the string was pulled tight to hold the two parts together. The tail of the string was then used to sling the device into the air. When it came down and hit the ground, a satisfactory bang was produced.

However, satisfaction is a relative term, and it was not long before certain boys started to experiment with ways of increasing the volume of the bang by using other explosives, such as red match heads or mixtures containing Potassium Chlorate, which was freely available in small quantities from any chemist at the time. The limitation was in the amount of explosive that could be packed into the small bomb, and it soon became apparent that more ambitious devices were required. These proved to be a pairs of large bolts screwed into a single nut, which effectively changed what had been a harmless toy into a dangerous and illegal device, capable of causing serious injury.

After one of these buried a half-inch bolt in the playground, (the other two parts were never found), the mere possession of such a device at school, became a caning offence.

One of the rougher playground pastimes was a modified game of leapfrog with two teams of boys. Starting with four boys, the first team would bend down and form a bridge ending at a brick wall. A member of the second team would take a short run and try to vault over the backs of the other boys to reach the wall. If successful, another boy would join the bridge and the vaulter would try again, adding boys to the bridge until the vaulter failed to reach the wall. After each attempt the members of the 'bridge' would chant a meaningless rhyme to the refrain of "London Bridge is Falling Down". It is not clear where this game originated, but it certainly seemed to be a hangover from the last century. It was discouraged, due to the possibility of an overenthusiastic vaulter's head or face coming into sharp contact with the wall at the end of the bridge.

Another centuries old game, was 'Conkers'. In the autumn, the boys gathered Horse Chestnuts, or 'Conkers'. These were individually threaded on a length of string or a bootlace. Taking turns, one boy would hold his Conker out at arms length, while the other competitor would try to smash it with his own. If the first attempt failed, the roles would be reversed, and the game would continue until one or the other Conker was destroyed. Various means were tried to 'toughen-up' Conkers, by baking them, or soaking them in vinegar, but none of these treatments seemed to be very effective.

From time to time the knuckles of the target player would receive a painful rap from his opponent's Conker. This was shrugged off as part of the game, and could be avoided to some extent by the use of gloves, but the very suggestion of such a thing is enough to cause nightmares to today's perpetrators of unwanted cosseting regulations. The game if seen at all these days has been banned in many schools.

A feature of the school during the coldest days, when the playgrounds were covered with frost, were the long ice slides made by the boys. Despite threats of draconian punishments by Tim the headmaster, this practice was never successfully stamped out. The caretaker would throw sand on the slides to avoid accidents when people came in the evenings for adult classes, but the next morning they would be started again in a different place.

In the girls' playground, less rough pastimes were to be found. Skipping ropes were very popular at the time, either used by individual girls, or with a longer rope and several girls participating. Games with tennis balls were also popular, and hopscotch, marked with chalk on the playground was a year round pastime. Gymnastic exercises were also popular, these being mainly cartwheels and hand-stands. The hand-stands were normally done against a wall. Before doing these exercises, the girls would tuck their skirts in to the top of their dark blue flannel knickers with elastic on the legs. These were universally worn and were the only type of underwear available to young girls at this time. They were so unattractive that they hardly drew a glance from any of the boys.

SCHOOL UNIFORMS.

During the late forties and early fifties, there was no compulsory school uniform at Alperton School. Indeed, many of the boys were wearing handed down clothes from older brothers, or coats made by their Mother out of ex-Army uniform material. In wintertime, some of the taller boys might be seen wearing an old Army greatcoat. Knitted Balaclava helmets and gloves were also commonly seen during the winter months, along with the occasional leather pilot's helmet. A rare status symbol would be an ex-Navy submariners white roll necked sweater

It might fairly be said, that when the whistle blew in the morning for the boys to line up for classes, the sight was more reminiscent of an East European refugee camp than a school playground.

It should be remembered that new clothes were still rationed, expensive, and in short supply. Any suggestion that a school uniform should be compulsory would not have been well received by many of the less advantaged parents from the Lyon Park and Alperton council estates. Although school caps and jackets were available at Rumbell's School Outfitters, in Wembley High Street, they were rarely seen in the playgrounds.

Boys at the time would customarily wear short trousers for the first and possibly second year at Alperton. It was a memorable time for a boy to arrive at school for the first time in long trousers.

For footwear, boots were almost universally worn, many of them home repaired, with Blakey's steel studs in the soles, and steel half-moon plates in the toes and heels.

Footwear was also rationed and hard to come by at the time. Even raw leather for home repairs was hard to find, so the hobnails and studs were considered essential to stretch the life of boots at the time. The studs had the added advantage of enabling the wearer to take a short run, and slide on the playground, often leaving a shower of sparks behind.

EXTRA CURRICULAR ACTIVITIES.

On the centenary of the 1851 Great Exhibition, the government decided to hold the Festival of Britain. The original exhibition in Hyde Park, featured the Crystal Palace, and was constructed in only nine months from planning stage to opening.

The site chosen for the 1951 Festival, was on the bank of the Thames at Battersea, an area noted at the time for its power station, run down industrial facilities, and unimproved bomb sites left over from the war. Officially known as the South Bank Exhibition, the project was not overly ambitious, the main buildings being a large domed structure known as the Dome of Discovery, and the Festival Hall, which remains today, a popular venue for art films and live musical performances.

The old shot tower, resembling a fat factory chimney, which had somehow survived the Blitz, was tarted-up as part of the site, but with no particular part to play, other than its possible date of construction being around 1850s.

There was also a modern art exhibit known as the 'Skylon', consisting of a cigar shaped object held in suspension by steel cables terminating in three steel posts. It was said that the most frequently asked question by visitors was: "What is it? What does it do?" When told that it was simply a Work of Art they would walk away, shaking their heads with a bemused expression.

A good deal of time at the school was spent publicizing the event. At the time we were in Miss Parson's class, and various class projects were started. A lucky few were also taken with school parties to visit the exhibition. Despite all the efforts of the teachers to drum up patriotic enthusiasm, the most popular part of the festival was the funfair in the adjacent festival gardens, and the firework displays.

POP'S.

Between the school gate and Wally & Geoff Lloyds motorcycle showroom, was 'Pop's', a seedy coffee shop which sold ice-lollies to the pupils during playtime breaks. Pop would drum up business with a 'something for nothing' queue. The first few in line would receive free (and inferior) ice-lollies, while the remainder would have to part with a few pennies. The content of these treats was problematical, but it is unlikely that fruit juice of any kind figured in the formula. The chemical colouring was inclined to stain the mouth of the consumer for the rest of the day. The business collapsed after Pop was found to be recycling lolly sticks, collected from the pavements and gutters of Ealing Road, and was prosecuted by the public health authorities.

AFTERNOONS AT THE PICTURES.

One of the more positive aspects of the austerity policy of the post war government was a limitation on the import of films from America. This encouraged the British studios to produce some landmark films. Many of the best Ealing productions were made at this time.

The school would occasionally march the pupils up to the Odeon Cinema, in Wembley High Street, next door to the General Post Office, to see films that were considered to have particular educational merit.

Some of the classics that come to mind were: Great Expectations, Oliver Twist, Hamlet, and Scott of the Antarctic. These episodes provided a welcome break from the dull routine of lessons, and were one of the more productive ideas to be spawned by the MoE.

After the film show, the pupils were allowed to go directly home, and since the film would normally finish about an hour earlier than classes, this could be counted as an added bonus to end an enjoyable afternoon.

2010. nearly completed.this amazing Hindu Temple now occupies the site of the old Alperton Secondary Modern school.

HOME LIFE

WASHING DAY.

Omo adds brightness to whiteness you see.

Early commercial TV jingle.

People who have grown up with modern washing machines and tiled bathrooms would have found life decidedly Spartan in the forties and fifties. In fact it would be fair to say that the average housewife of today, accustomed to disposable nappies and labour saving appliances would be horrified by what her counterpart of those times would accept as normal.

Laundry detergents were unknown in the forties, but a variety of other things were used on washing day. This included soap flakes, available either in cardboard boxes, or sold loose by the pound at the ironmongers, or stores such as Robinsons in Ealing Road. Washing soda was also sold by the pound, as well as large blocks of hard yellow washing soap. Another product was laundry 'Blue', which supposedly made whites whiter. Parazone bleach was also popular.

The laundry was generally done in a galvanized iron washing tub, using a corrugated scrubbing board, and a stiff bristle scrubbing brush. While most houses in Wembley had piped hot water, either from an Ideal Boiler, or a gas fired Geyser, the less fortunate housewife in older properties would have to heat the water in saucepans on the gas stove.

Having washed the clothes, they were taken for wringing to the mangle, which was a hand operated machine with two rollers that squeezed the water out of the cloth, a task which is today performed by a spin cycle in the washing machine. The mangle could either be the old Victorian design, with a cast iron frame, and a system of gears sounding remarkably like a tram, or the more modern lightweight variety mounted on a tubular steel stand.

The partially-dry laundry would then be hung out to dry on the washing line, supported by a prop to keep them well above the ground. This system worked well in summertime, when the air was fairly clean, but in winter, with the regular smogs, a white sheet could become grey with soot before it dried. After washing, all clothes were generally ironed, and most housewives had an electric iron and an ironing board. Some people however, still used the old fashioned irons which were heated on the gas stove.

For those who could afford it, Wembley Laundry offered a home pick-up and delivery service. Located in the India Pavilion on the old exhibition site, the laundry operated two Albion lorries, built in the early twenties. These relics were used until the fifties when they were finally retired, probably for safety reasons at the behest of the police. The laundry also ran a pair of more modern streamlined vans of unusual design.

Most men wore collar detached shirts at the time, and another enterprising company also situated on the Estate operating a home delivery service was Collars, which would deliver a weeks supply of clean starched collars in a box, and pick up the soiled ones.

In the early fifties, the first 'Bagwash' laundry opened in Ealing Road next to the junction with Chaplin Road. People could take their laundry in a pillowcase, and collect it the same day. It was damp, ready for ironing, but all of the hard work had been done. Regular customers were later provided with special canvas laundry bags. Soiled nappies were unacceptable at the bagwash, so the nauseating chore of washing them still had to be performed by the housewife.

HOME DELIVERIES.

Any old rags, bottles or bones ?

Totters cry

Up until the late fifties, bread and milk were delivered daily to households around Wembley. In areas close to the dairy depot, milk delivery would be by pedestrian steered electric, battery driven carts. Two varieties of cart were used, one being controlled by a control shaft at the front, and another by an arrangement resembling bicycle handlebars at the back. Since these were regarded as powered vehicles by the road traffic acts, a special driving license was required, and the milkman or baker's delivery man had to take a special driving test to obtain this. The United Dairies, Co-op, and Express Dairies also used horse drawn milk carts to service the more distant customers. All of the main dairies would deliver milk either in Half Pint, Pint or Quart bottles. The United Dairy bottles had a broad neck, and were sealed by a cardboard disk, pressed in when the bottle was filled. A small tab enabled the consumer to pull out the cardboard cap. Express Dairy bottles had a narrower neck, and were sealed by an aluminium cap.

The milkman would normally leave the full bottles on the doorstep, and collect the empties. If the housewife did not take the full bottles in promptly, it would not be long before the local blue-tits would arrive, to peck away at the bottle cap to get at the cream on top of the milk. In those days the milk was not homogenized or otherwise interfered with, and the cream would gather at the top of the contents. It was necessary to shake the bottle before using the milk, or if one preferred, the cream could be poured on to breakfast porridge or cereal. Special sterilized milk was available in snap top bottles, which was similar in taste to watered down tinned evaporated milk. Mainly consumed by T.B. sufferers this product could be purchased in several grocery stores around Wembley.

Later, the horse drawn milk and baker's carts were replaced by silent running electric vehicles. Also around that time, the United Dairies milk bottles were changed to the narrower necked version, sealed by a thin aluminium cap, the colour of which indicated the contents of the bottle. Normal milk would have a silver top, and extra rich Jersey milk would have a Gold top. Un-pasteurized milk was not generally available, but carried a green cap. Quart bottles were no longer sold. Unlike the few remaining milk rounds men of today, who carry an assortment of food and dairy products, only milk was delivered.

The baker's van, also horse drawn would deliver freshly baked bread, either white or brown, all crusty, fresh and unwrapped. Sliced bread was not available, and wrapped supermarket 'Bread' such as Mothers Pride was a distant nightmare.

By the fifties, coal deliveries, which had also been by horse drawn vehicles, drawn by two considerably more robust horses than the baker or milkman, had given way to lorries. With the clip clop of the horse drawn carts, replaced by the quiet whine of the electric variety, accompanied by the clink of bottles in the steel wire milk crates, perhaps the greatest loss was to the amateur gardeners, who were no longer able to collect a bucket of horse droppings from the road every day.

Henceforth, only the rag and bone men would be using horse drawn carts on the streets of Wembley. Their call of 'Any old ragbone' was a familiar sound up to the mid fifties.

Coal deliveries were also part of life in the forties. All houses had a coal store or cellar, and often two stores, one for coal and the other for coke. Coke was a by-product of the town gas works. At that time the entire supply of gas in the country was produced by baking coal in the local Gasworks, and huge gas-holders, known to the public as 'Gasometers' were a common sight. Fortunately the two nearest gasworks to Wembley were situated at Kensal Rise, and Hanwell, so the town was spared the stench and air pollution produced by these facilities. The *Gas Light & Coke Company* used steam driven lorries using coke as fuel. Coke was relatively inexpensive but would not burn well in an open fire grate. However, many homes had an 'Ideal' Boiler in the kitchen, which was designed to burn coke, and any kitchen rubbish such as cabbage stalks etc, while at the same time providing hot water for the house.

The coalman wore a round leather cap, with a wide leather apron at the back to protect his neck and shoulders. Coal came in bags of one and two hundredweight, the larger ones requiring considerable strength on the part of the coalman to carry it. It was generally the job of one of the younger members of the family to count the number of bags delivered. Ten of the larger bags made up the usual delivery of one ton.

Tony recalls one occasion when the one of the coalmen tripped and fell onto the coal pile with the sack on his back, and was unable to move until the second man came and pulled it off him.

Due to inept management of the coal industry by the government, there were frequent coal shortages at this time.

The other weekly home visitors were the dustmen, who at the time wore the same type of leather cap as the coalmen. The standard size dustbin held about 50 gallons, and was made of galvanized steel. When half full of ashes and other rubbish it would also weigh in at over 100 pounds. It had to be lifted from the ground, unlike the coal sacks, which were taken from the tailgate of a cart.

The dustcarts used by Wembley council up to the early fifties were pre-war Crossley vehicles with solid tyres. The rear of the dustcart was covered by half round sliding panels, which could be closed when the vehicle was moving to minimize the loss of cargo, and reduce its inevitable smell.

During the war, the council placed dustbins on every street corner for the collection of kitchen waste, to be converted into pig food to help the war effort. In Wembley, the practice continued after the war, and the collected contents of these 'pigbins' were cooked at the council dump at Alperton Lane, to produce a black tarry substance sold as 'Wembley Pudding' to farmers. There was a summertime problem of breeding flies and a smell that had to be experienced to be believed, which finally put an end to the practice in the mid fifties.

Another home visitor of the forties and fifties was the District Nurse, who, with a characteristic dark blue uniform, and a Raleigh or Rudge Auto-cycle, was a common sight going her rounds in Wembley. It was customary at the time for women to give birth at home, except where serious complications were expected. The District Nurse would act as midwife when the time came.

A somewhat less than welcome visitor was the council Sanitary Inspector, an imposing figure with a peaked cap, whose job it was to inspect drains and unsanitary living conditions. During and directly after the war, he had plenty of work to do in Wembley, particularly in overcrowded boarding houses, which catered for itinerant labourers.

In the fifties, when war time rationing finally ended mobile ice cream vans appeared for the first time. Replacing the old pre-war, Walls Ice Cream "Stop me and buy one" tricycles, these vans would announce their arrival with amplified musical box chimes. In addition to ice cream they also sold fruit ice-lollies. They would usually call when the children were out of school, often as many as three times a day.

Also in the early fifties a number of enterprising mobile greengrocers appeared on the scene using old army lorries. Most housewives walked to the shops every day with a shopping basket, and the prospect of not having to carry back a stone of potatoes with her other groceries must have been welcomed with open arms.

The more affluent shoppers could have their groceries delivered from the shop by a boy riding a purpose made delivery bicycle having a small size front wheel and a large box carrier in front of the handlebars. The larger grocery stores such as Sainsbury's provided this service.

The Post Office was very efficient and reliable in those days. In addition to making a morning and afternoon letter delivery every day, including Christmas Day, a letter posted on one day would be guaranteed for delivery the following day. Also, if a letter was posted early, addressed locally, it would be delivered the same day.

Telegrams were delivered by young boys, known as telegraph boys, wearing a blue uniform and a pill box hat, usually riding heavy, red Post Office issue bicycles. Later, the old bicycles were to be replaced by BSA Bantam two stroke motorcycles, also painted bright Post Office red.

After school hours, children aged thirteen or older were permitted to supplement their pocket money by delivering newspapers door to door. The amount of payment received by these delivery boys, varied between four and six shillings for a seven day week, depending on the size of the round.

Another regular visitor to the growing number of council estates was the rent collector. Derek lived on the Farm Avenue estate where the rent was collected every Monday by a Mrs. Benjamin, a no nonsense woman who walked from door to door collecting the rent money in a leather satchel. At the time, it was a point of honour for families to pay their rent even if money was desperately short. This same woman would also carry out an annual inspection of each house and woe betides any tenant not adhering strictly to the rules of occupancy. These rules were laid down in the municipal housing handbook issued to every council tenant. After completing her round she would return by bus to the town hall. The rest of the week she would be collecting rent from the other estates. It seems incredible by today's standards, that in all the years she collected rent money in the late forties and fifties, she was never the victim of a mugging.

Today the idea of a house inspection would represent an unwarranted intrusion on the privacy of the individual. However, it should be remembered that many of the families living on council estates were relocated from bombed out slum dwellings, and while the majority of tenants took great pride in their new homes and gardens, there were a very small minority who did not, and if these proved to be incorrigible, they would be evicted by the council and a more deserving family installed in the house.

A long forgotten door-to-door service was the delivery of soft drinks by the Corona Man.

This company, located in the Abbey Estate, near the North Circular Road sold soft drinks in a returnable bottle with a spring snap top. Flavours offered were lemonade, limeade, dandelion & burdock, cream soda, ginger beer, and orangeade. Price was sixpence for a pint bottle. Door to door deliveries were made twice weekly by lorries in the more distant areas, and by hand drawn electric trucks in the Lyon Park estates.

It is a tragedy that this service did not survive, but soft drink suppliers generally have found that it is more profitable to make the customer buy the bottle as well as its contents, and also pay for its disposal, be it glass or plastic.

After the war, home deliveries of paraffin heating oil were started by Aladdin Pink, and Esso Blue. These products fuelled the effective, if malodorous oil heaters, which became popular in the early fifties, and were the cause of many house fires.

Paraffin oil was a by-product of the numerous town gas works existing at the time. In later years it was replaced by kerosene. Many people may remember the commercials for these products on the fledgling ITV television channels.

Finally there was the home collection and delivery by Wembley Laundry, and Collars, mentioned in an earlier chapter.

FOG AND SMOG.

"I couldn't see a hand in front of me, when Bang! I walked into a lamp-post and got myself a bloody nose."

Wembley Resident, 1952

London has always been subject to fogs. Situated in a basin, between two ranges of hills, autumn and wintertime fogs tended to fill up the basin, trapped by a temperature inversion layer above. The expansion of London in medieval times, and the widespread use of 'Sea Coal' shipped down from Newcastle saw the birth of the choking 'London Peculiars' mentioned by Dickens.

In the forties and fifties, the November and December fogs were a regular feature of life in Wembley. At the low point by Wembley fire station, Tony used to stand outside his house and watch the trolleybus drivers being guided by the conductor walking ahead of the bus carrying a torch. There would often be a line of other traffic following the bus, and there were many stories of hopelessly lost drivers of cars following the trolleybuses into the Stonebridge Depot.

Almost without exception, the vast numbers of houses in and around Wembley were heated by open-hearth fireplaces burning soft coal. The amount of pollution caused by these fireplaces could readily be gauged by the build-up of thick black soot in the chimneys, which had to be regularly swept. This soot, if allowed to accumulate would often itself catch fire, producing a thick foul smelling white smoke which would blanket the area.

Things came to a head early in December 1952 when, as a result of gross mismanagement on the part of the government, there was a serious coal shortage in the country. As a panic reaction, the authorities released thousands of tons of coal dust, optimistically called 'Nutty Slack', for public consumption. This coal dust, when added to a fire produced nothing but smoke, and its widespread distribution in London coincided with a static weather pattern, trapping the pollution and fog for five days in the London basin.

On 5th December, Tony, riding his bike along the Harrow Road in Kensal Rise, from Paddington, noticed a dark brown sky on the horizon ahead. By the time he got home, visibility was down to a few yards. Over the next few days things got steadily worse, and the fog, heavy with sulphur dioxide as well as particulate matter, started to aggravate bronchial disorders. People forced to go outdoors took to wearing surgical masks, which were quickly renamed 'Smog Masks'. Others would wear a scarf over their mouth and nose. At one point, it was possible to stand directly under the street lamps in Chaplin Road, and only see a very faint glow from above. Cinemas were forced to close when the air inside became too thick to show the film.

Walking in a pea-souper was truly like being immersed in pea soup. Sounds were completely muffled; even the brightest torch didn't penetrate the murk. The illumination just bounced back at you. It was damp almost to the point of a drizzle, but worst of all would be the choking air that you breathed in. Your clothes when you reached home would be filthy.

Derek caught the number 18 bus at the Wembley triangle to go home after work. The ride to Barham Park and then a short walk up Chaplin Road to Farm Avenue normally took twenty minutes. After an hour sitting on the bus, which travelled no more than a few yards, he decided to get off and walk. Once past the dimly lit shops in the High Road, he had to walk with his right foot in the gutter on a course he reckoned would take him to the left turn into Chaplin Road. This in fact took him into the fire station. He carried on regardless and found himself in the Territorial Army barracks on the corner of Linthorpe Avenue. It took him a half an hour to get back on course again, only to get lost once more. Eventually, only by knocking on house doors and asking where he was, did he get home. The journey took a total of three hours from leaving work.

When the weather pattern changed on 9th December, and the wind finally dispersed the smog, the shocking facts became clear. Four thousand deaths, mainly of old people, finally rising to an estimated total of twelve thousand, were attributed to the disaster. Instead of calling for the resignation, or better still the public hanging of the Minister of Fuel and Power, the government went into defence and disinformation mode familiar to watchers of *Yes Minister* on TV.

With the realization that something had to be done to prevent a repetition of the great smog, the Clean Air Act of 1956 introduced smoke controlled areas. Each area had a date after which only smokeless fuel would be permitted. Government grants were awarded to enable householders to convert their existing fireplaces to burn smokeless fuel or coke. These alternative fuels were generally unpopular because they were more expensive than coal. A number of busybodies were employed by the government to walk the streets on the look-out for chimneys 'Uttering visible smoke', which would render the householder liable to a fine. These measures did little to reduce the amount of sulphur in the smog, but it did remove the larger problem of the smoke. By 1958 it was possible to stand on top of Horsenden Hill, and see the television mast at Crystal Palace on the far side of London. Previously this would have been impossible even under the best conditions. In 1968 a modification to the act required power stations to be moved away from cities, and factories burning fuel had to increase the height of their chimneys.

Although there was never a repeat of the killer smog, the steady increase in the volume of road traffic, and the replacement of the non-polluting trolleybus by smoke belching diesel buses and giant lorries, created an air quality problem possibly as bad, if not worse. The present day smog lasts all year instead of the first few winter months, an is undoubtedly the cause of many premature deaths each year.

NEWSPAPERS AND SCANDALS.

STARNEWSSTANDARD, CLASSIFIED RESULTS!

Wembley street news-vendors cry.

Memories of foggy November evenings, with people hurrying home from work, during the evening rush hour around 5.30 p.m., cause the authors to recall the hoarse cry of "Starnewstandard" from the newsvendor outside the Railway Hotel, together with the sound of the Trollybus silently swishing past the Ealing Road traffic lights, and the rattle of the diesel engine on the 83 Bus waiting to turn into Wembley High Road when the lights changed.

Before the days when television claimed thirty percent of the waking hours of the population, there was a flourishing newspaper industry in England. In addition to the daily newspapers, there were several evening papers, such as the

Evening News, Evening Standard and the Star, which carried the latest sports results, and would be sold in large numbers to people on their way home from work in the evenings. These evening newspapers generally had an early and a late edition, the first being available around 4 p.m. and home delivered by the paperboy, the late edition being sold by street news-vendors.

Daily newspapers included the Daily Herald and the Daily Mirror, both left-leaning publications, and the Daily Express, Daily Mail, and Daily Telegraph supporting the Conservative and Liberal parties. The Communist party's Daily Worker had a more limited circulation, generally being sold on street corners by party members rather than on news-stands. Compared to what are generally sold as newspapers today, these daily sheets were in fact worthy of the name, and actually contained news. The closest thing to modern publications such as The Sun, or the Mirror, was a little weekly trivia magazine known as Tit-Bits. Even so, the comparison would be less than fair, since Tit-Bits did not publish pictures of naked women in an attempt to boost flagging circulation.

The size of the newspaper was a good guide to the target readership. The more serious newspapers, such as The Times were large format publications, aimed at the more affluent members of society, and generally had a well-used correspondence column filled by letters from retired army generals, deploring the way the country was going, and others anxious to report hearing the first Cuckoo of the summer. The Times crossword puzzle then as now, was not to be attempted by the faint-hearted. Tabloid-sized newspapers such as the Daily Mirror which enjoyed the largest circulation at the time, invited readers letters to "The Old Codgers". The Mirror also carried a full page of comic strips and cartoons, featuring among others, 'Jane', 'Garth', 'Just Jake', 'Useless Eustace' etc. Two particularly effective political cartoonists during the war were 'Zec', and 'Vicky'

During the war there was a paper shortage, and the number of pages allowed by newspapers, was sharply reduced. The larger format papers were limited to four pages, while tabloid sized publications such as The Mirror were allowed up to ten pages.

In order to compensate for this reduction, the publishers reduced the print size to the point where it became difficult to read without glasses.

The paper shortage also produced a number of innovative ways to use old newspapers. Where normally they would be used for firelighters, or perhaps for wrapping fish & chips, many were now cut up into squares and threaded on a wire to be used as make shift toilet paper when the real thing was not available, as was often the case.

In Wembley there were a number of spots favored by newspaper vendors. The entrances to Wembley Central station and Alperton station had daily pitches, as well as a regular spot on the corner of Ealing Road, by the Railway Hotel. In addition there were a large number of tobacconists selling newspapers around the town.

The Wembley News and the Wembley Observer were local papers. The Wembley News, published weekly, dealt with local issues and was published and printed at the Triangle in Wembley. The Wembley Observer was published by King and Hutchings in Uxbridge, who also produced the Harrow Observer, and other local papers each Friday.

The Sunday newspapers were also very popular with the reading public, particularly the News of the World, otherwise known as the "Crime and Crumpet", specializing in lurid accounts of cases in the criminal courts, with particular emphasis to scandals touching on scoutmasters, clergymen, and members of the aristocracy. The Sunday Pictorial was less inclined to specialize in the more lurid news, and was noted for its gardening page.

From time to time, the routine cases of small time crime, homosexuality, and carnal knowledge of under-age girls, were pre-empted by particularly gruesome murder trials, which would generally last for several weeks and enjoyed an avid readership.

A celebrated murder trial in 1946 of Neville Heath, who murdered two women, after sexually torturing them in a bizarre manner, was a particularly toothsome example.

Heath was brought to trial on 24th September 1946, was found guilty and hanged on 16th October the same year. The height of the 'drop' was duly reported in the newspapers.

Another big windfall for the press, was the so-called Acid Bath murders by John George Haig, who came to trial on 18th July 1949. Haig had murdered at least six victims between 1944 and 1949 when he was arrested reportedly dissolving the bodies of his victims in drums of sulphuric acid, thinking that an actual body was required before murder charges could be made. He was mistaken, and was duly hanged on 10th August 1949. A particularly gruesome aspect of this case was Haig's claim to have drunk a glass of the blood of each of his victims before consigning them to the acid bath. The Daily Mirror had a field day reporting court proceedings.

Perhaps the last of the mass-murder cases of the fifties was the case of John Reginald Christie. The murders came to the attention of the police, when a West Indian immigrant, inspecting a flat he had just rented, discovered what appeared to be a cupboard that had been wallpapered over. Poking a hole in the paper, he peered through the hole to find the face of a dead woman looking back at him. It was said that the unfortunate man ran for almost two miles before calming down enough to contact the authorities. A search uncovered four bodies of women in the house, and a further two buried in the garden. The case was complicated by the fact that Timothy Evans, an acquaintance of Christie had been convicted of murdering his wife and child, and was subsequently hanged. Christie finally confessed to this murder and was hanged at Pentonville Prison on 15th July 1953.

Another notable case, which served to dramatically boost the circulation of the Sunday newspapers, was the trial of Lord Montagu of Beaulieu and two others for homosexual offences in 1954. The trial dragged on for some time, and all the old Oscar Wilde jokes were dusted off and adapted, for Lord Montague, as well as a parody on the 'Twelve Days of Christmas' song. The British public of the forties and fifties truly enjoyed a good scandal.

Wembley had its own home grown murder case, when George Edward Crick pushed a younger schoolboy into the river Brent. At the time, his arrest caused a sensation in the press, he being the youngest murder suspect of the century. Mention is made of this case in the chapter on Alperton School.

A Hornby 0 gauge electric Loco. Below. A London single deck bus, constructed from a number nine Meccano set. The post-war red and green colours have always been our favorite

BEFORE COMPUTER GAMES

TOYS WE PLAYED WITH.

Hornby trains are loads of fun, every minute spent playing with Hornby trains is brim full of thrills and enjoyment. Hornby trains are strong pulling, long running, tested and guaranteed.

Meccano Magazine

In the days before the television screen came to dominate the lives of children, they had to rely on a facility that everybody is born with, but which today they have less opportunity to exercise. We refer of course to imagination. Many of the popular toys of the pre-television era were designed to stimulate the imagination of children, and the majority of the more popular boys toys were construction kits of one kind or another.

When real toys were not available the imagination can turn a stick into a sword, or a rifle, a piece of string can turn the stick into a whip etc. A great prize during and shortly after the war would be the wheels off an old pram, which with a short plank of wood and an old box could be made into a racing car. If pram wheels were unavailable, old ball bearings would serve. Ball bearings could also be pressed into service as the wheels of a home-made scooter. An old bicycle wheel stripped of spokes, became a hoop, or with a sack stretched across it, a net for fishing in the canal. Girls might use a piece of cast-off cloth to make dolls clothes.

Modern children no longer have to resort to these measures.

The traditional toyshop has generally gone the way of the Dodo, being replaced by huge outlets offering an ocean of bright plastic trash and mind rotting video games. However, there used to be two real toyshops in Wembley. One of these was in Ealing Road opposite Douglas Avenue. It was owned by an elderly couple, he looking like a double for Mr Pastry, a comedian of the fifties. Apart from traditional toys, dolls etc., even throughout the war, model aeroplane kits, Balsa-wood, and general model-making supplies were available from this little shop, as well as components for model railway layouts. This business changed hands on their retirement in the fifties, and became Bullens Toy Shop.

The second dedicated toy-shop, was a few doors down from the Majestic cinema in Wembley High Road. This shop catered for the more affluent customers, offering dolls houses, toy rocking-horses, pedal cars and suchlike, as well as the traditional smaller toys and board games.

In addition to these toyshops, a department store called Arthurs, at the top of Ealing Road, had a small toy department, which was a reliable source of Rupert Bear books and children's annuals from popular comics, as well as the Daily Mail annual for boys and girls.

Due to wartime shortages, the manufacture of metal toys was banned in 1941, and it was not until 1947 to 1948 that small quantities again became available. Derek's Mother, hearing a rumor in 1947 that Triang Minic clockwork cars were on sale, rushed up to the toyshop in the High Road, and bought for four shillings and ninepence, a red and green tinplate clockwork powered lorry. It wasn't until 1948 that he got a number 5 Meccano set, purchased at Green and Barnes, radio and electrical dealers in Ealing Road, opposite the Chequers public house. This store had one of the two franchise agencies in Wembley to sell Meccano products, including Hornby trains and Dinky toys. The other was Wally Kilminster at the Triangle. Neither of these were toyshops as such.

CONSTRUCTION KITS.

Boys like to make things, metal construction kits such as Meccano, perhaps being the most popular in our own youth.

Invented by Frank Hornby in Liverpool as a toy for his children, it became famous as Meccano, a toy which enabled models to be built, changed or dismantled at will, from a simple child's toy, to an advanced and complex engineering project.

Starting with the basic number 1 set, a child could hope to acquire an extension kit each birthday or Christmas, to bring it up to the next number. For example, a 1A set would turn a number 1 into a number 2 and so forth. The final monster set, which very few could hope for, was the number 10, in its wooden cabinet. Derek did finally, late in life, build his collection up to a number ten, and was able to construct some very fine and complex models.

A cheaper copy, sometimes called the poor boy's Meccano was Trix, a smaller and more limited system made in aluminium. Trix could be bought at Woolworths for two shillings a packet, which would only contain a few components. It would require a lot of these packets to make anything ambitious.

An American copy of Meccano, sold as Erector, became very popular on the other side of the Atlantic. They were made in the USA by Gilbert toys from 1910 to the 1960's. This was a major system, some parts of which were interchangable with Meccano, which led to Gilbert becoming involved in serious patent litigation with Hornby. Gilbert also manufactured American flyer model railroad trains in S & 0 gauges, two-rail electric trains that rivaled the famous Lionel three rail system. Some of the above American products were on sale in the pre-war years at the big London stores such as Gamages.

Juneero was a metal construction toy built around a hand operated lever tool mounted on a baseplate. It included cutting shears for rods, cutting shears for metal strips, a die for threading rods, a bending jig for bars and a punch for perforating metal, plus a vice to hold rods for-screw cutting. In 1940, a number 1 outfit cost twelve shillings and sixpence, and a number 2 set cost twenty-five shillings.

Dinky Builder was aimed at the future Meccano owner. These simple outfits for the very young, consisting of square, triangular and oblong metal plates, fitted together with rods, which had to be pushed into hinges on the sides of the metal pieces.

Besides the 'Nuts & Bolts' metal construction sets, there were a number of building kits available using bricks of one kind or another from which model houses could be built.

The Bayco system used Bakelite bricks which were held together with metal rods and ties to make houses and other buildings.

The innovation of the Brick Player system, was that buildings could be constructed with miniature bricks and mortar. The set came with bricks and a little trowel, and a flour paste which was mixed with water. Finished buildings when they became redundant, could be dismantled by soaking in water, and the bricks used again.

A similar building game was called "Lotts Bricks". Advertised as a constructional toy of unique charm - providing endless amusement for boys and girls of all ages, it was a building kit using stone building bricks and printed cardboard roofs. They were manufactured in Watford by a company that also sold chemistry sets.

Yet another system, was Minibrix Rubber Building Blocks, which had moulded holes and projections, similar to today's Lego, making buildings very rigid and durable.

All of the foregoing building kits were made to a scale of 7mm to one foot, making the buildings suitable for Hornby and other 0 gauge model railway layouts.

Dinky Toys. Die-cast cars and aeroplanes, military and commercial vehicles made by Meccano started to re-appear in the windows of Green & Barnes and Wally Kilminster in around late 1946-47, and enjoyed their best years of sales up until the appearance of other die-cast toys such as matchbox models in the late fifties. Dinky Supertoys, which were larger, more detailed and expensive, were out of the pocket money range and more in the birthday or Christmas present category.

TOY TRAINS.

After Meccano's success, Frank Hornby manufactured his own range of British 0 gauge trains in the 1920's. These wonderful, colorful tinplate electric trains and accessories would have been only for the well-to-do collector, but soon, cheaper and equally charming clockwork powered Hornby train sets were also available.

In 1938, Hornby introduced Hornby Dublo, 00 gauge, a much more realistic looking train set, being half the size of 0 gauge, enabling much more ambitious and realistic layouts to be achieved. Sadly, after the war the larger 0 gauge trains were no longer manufactured, and with smaller houses and rooms, the 00 gauge was the in thing, although a limited range of the 0 gauge clockwork sets and accessories aimed at the younger market were on sale up to the 1960's.

Not classed as toy trains, and out of the price range of most children Basset Lowke were model makers of renown. Manufacturing live steam, electric, and clockwork powered scale model locomotives, these were for the serious collector, and owners of large and outdoor layouts.

Rovex Plastics of Richmond was a newcomer to the toy train market in Christmas 1951 which saw an electric train set selling at thirty nine shillings and elevenpence at Marks & Spencer in Wembley High Road. This was comprised of a Pacific-type engine, and two carriages, running on a two rail 00 gauge track. The set was made from injection-moulded plastic and very finely detailed. Power was supplied by a battery box containing four U2 torch batteries. Its downfall was the unavailability of any extra track or rolling stock, thus committing the train to chase its rear end forever on the small oval track provided. Rovex was finally bought out by Triang, another 00 gauge train manufacturer, who also bought out Hornby/Meccano in 1961.

OTHER TOYS.

Toy cap pistols and cowboy costumes were also popular with boys, but again they were relatively expensive and reserved for birthdays and Christmas presents.

Smaller popular toys included pea-shooters. However, dried peas were in short supply due to rationing, and during the late forties, short lengths of glass tubing were used as pea-shooters using pearl barley as ammunition. Home-made catapults were always popular with boys, but suitable elastic was very hard to find, and the catapults were subject to confiscation by teachers or the police if the owner was caught using one.

Air pistols and rifles were the ultimate prize, but were unavailable to boys under thirteen years of age. The least expensive were air pistols by Diana, which were loaded by pushing the telescopic barrel in. They were not particularly accurate due to the spring recoil, but were popular. Webley produced a range of three air pistols, the ultimate being the Webley Senior, which was available with either a .177, or .22 calibre barrel. Both BSA and Webley produced fine quality rifles, the less expensive being cocked by bending the barrel down, and the top of the line having an under lever cocking mechanism, the pellets being loaded via a tap arrangement. These also offered both .177 and .22 models.

Fivestones, a game possibly dating back to Roman times, was popular with both boys and girls. Various other games were played with glass marbles of different sizes.

In contrast to those of the boys, the toys that girls played with did not change a great deal over the years.

Girls are very fond of dressing up, and it seems that the nurses uniform has retained its popularity over the years, as well as dolls of various kinds. Dolls houses, toy stoves and tea services, typewriters, and the ubiquitous skipping ropes.

Whipping tops were also more popular with girls than with boys.

After the war, such things as pedal cars, Mickey Mouse tricycles, and larger tricycles made by various bicycle manufacturers became available, albeit in limited numbers, as well as child-size two wheel bicycles.

An annual event was the schoolboys and girls exhibition at the Horticultural Hall and later the Olympia in the fifties, where all the latest toys were on display.

HOBBIES.

Meccano engineering for boys. Every boy is happiest when he is inventing, creating and constructing -That is why boys still find Meccano the most fascinating hobby in the world.

Meccano Magazine

During the forties and fifties, most boys and many girls had a hobby of one sort or another. Some boys had several hobbies, and were always busy building or collecting something.

A popular indoor and outdoor pursuit was the construction of flying model aeroplanes, generally purchased from Wally Kilminster on the Wembley Triangle, or the toyshop in Ealing Road opposite Douglas Avenue. These models, built with loving care by Tony, seldom survived their maiden flight. Many of the flying models were simply gliders, and while the instructions with the kit were generally adequate, they lacked information on trimming the completed model for flight. More ambitious models had a propeller driven by elastic bands passing through the length of the plane's fuselage. These had to be wound up by hand anticlockwise before each flight, which would generally be of short duration.

Miniature single-cylinder diesel engines were available for longer flights and larger models, and ran on ether mixed with a small quantity of castor oil. Once started, the engine could be adjusted to full power with a compression screw in the cylinder head.

These little engines made by such companies as Frog were far too expensive for the average young aero-modeller, although the occasional old second-hand one would show up at school. The starting procedure was to flick the propeller round with the forefinger, with the engine compression reduced. Newcomers to the art quickly learned to wear a leather glove while doing this. If one was lucky the engine would start and the compression could be increased for maximum power (and noise). However this was rarely the case and Tony remembers spending an hour fruitlessly trying to start an older engine which he had swapped in the school playground. He never succeeded in getting it to run.

Model jet engines were also available, the simplest being the Jetex, which was basically a little light alloy rocket, running on small slugs of compressed fuel, which was ignited by a thin fuse. These small engines would only run for a few seconds, but were relatively inexpensive and several model kits were designed specially for them.

It should be mentioned that the starter fuse was also very useful for home made fireworks. Jetex model engines are still made and sold in the UK today.

A far more determined jet engine was the Diana model pulse-jet. This was a miniature version of the engine that powered the V1 flying bombs. The fuel tank was pressurized with a bicycle pump, and once started it would run until the fuel was expended. Models powered by these engines would achieve speeds in excess of 100 m.p.h., and free flight operation was illegal for obvious reasons. It is said that the noise of these little jet engines could be heard as much as a mile away.

Radio-control was in its infancy in the forties and fifties, and no commercial equipment was available at the time. However, a few amateur constructors managed to devise simple and basic control systems. A licence was required from the Post Office to operate radio-controlled models

Non-flying scale model kits were also sold, but in the days before moulded plastic, far too much time and patience, not to mention skill, was required for us to produce an acceptable result.

For determined modelling enthusiasts, with good eyesight, and a set of Xacto knives, Micromodels produced a wide range of miniature model kits printed on cards, ranging from railway locomotives to famous buildings.

During the winter, hobbies were normally confined to indoor activities, other than by certain sports enthusiasts, and keen pike fishermen who would stand shivering all day beside river or lake, rarely catching anything other than a cold. Football and rugby enthusiasts would splash around on a muddy pitch in a freezing drizzle and convince themselves they were having a good time. Among the non-sporting community, winter pastimes included photography, chemistry sets, and construction of wireless sets as well as model making. Fretwork was also popular in the late forties and early fifties. A fretsaw and blades cost only a few shillings, and plywood could be salvaged from old tea chests. There was a magazine called *Hobbies Weekly* that published fretwork and carpentry designs.

Another popular hobbies publication that was greatly looked forward to was the Meccano Magazine. This little gem offered articles of general interest as well as details of small Meccano construction projects that were achievable by owners of fairly modest Meccano sets. The magazine also dealt with Hornby model trains showing pictures of ambitious layouts built by regular correspondents.

A Meccano set, mentioned in an earlier chapter, was something that almost every boy in the late forties owned at one time or another. Many never got beyond the starter kits, building simple projects. Boys with more well-to-do parents would build up their Meccano sets to the point where they were able to attempt some of the more difficult projects. The enthusiasm for this toy is never really lost: Derek finally acquired a number ten set in his late fifties, and was able to build models he remembered from his boyhood, including a single deck bus, and a Tiger Moth aeroplane.

Derek was also the first to dabble with photography, and constructed a makeshift darkroom in an upstairs clothes closet. Most families owned the popular and inexpensive pre-war Kodak Brownie box cameras, which produced two-and-a-half by three-and-a-half inch black-and white negatives. These negatives would produce excellent contact prints by use of a simple wooden or Bakelite printing frame. Developing trays, together with bottles of developer and Hypo fixer could be readily purchased at Boots Chemists for a modest price, together with the correct size printing paper, either 'Gaslight' for exposure in artificial light, or Bromide for sunlight.

Various contrast papers were available depending on the density of the negatives to be printed. Red safelights were also available at Boots, but more sophisticated equipment had to be obtained from Wallace Heaton in Bond Street.

However, our efforts seldom went beyond making copies of old family photographs, and with fingers stained brown by the chemicals we would hang up the pictures to dry like laundry, or lay them on a sheet of glass to dry with a gloss finish. Film was taken to the chemist's shop to be developed, because a developing tank was beyond our budget limitations, and the makeshift darkroom was not dark enough to safely

hand develop panchromatic film without fogging it. Colour film, although available was too expensive for most people, and the old simple cameras were unsuitable for colour photography

Around this time, in the late forties, Tony had been given a chemistry set as a Christmas present and developed an immediate interest. At the time, there was a second-hand bookshop opposite the Wembley police station, which had a large selection of old school chemistry books. He read these books from cover to cover and quickly discovered the limitations of his basic chemistry set. Fortunately, the toyshop in Ealing Road also sold glassware for chemistry sets, as well as test tubes filled with various chemicals. At the time it was also possible to buy a wide variety of chemicals over the counter at chemist shops. More complex glassware could also be obtained from Vicsons, in Pinner Road, Harrow

Several of the old chemistry books contained details of the manufacture of gunpowder and fireworks, which proved to be relatively easy to make at home if care was taken.

For setting off these home made fireworks, the fuse used in Jetex model aeroplane engines proved to be ideal, and a great deal of fun was had by all.

Although Tony had both the knowledge and the chemicals required to make high explosives, such as nitro glycerine, or Mercury Fulminate, he fortunately had sufficient common sense to refrain from trying to do so, which is one reason why he is able today to collaborate in the production of this 'little' book.

Another hobby shared by certain boys was the construction of simple radio sets. This usually began with the construction of crystal sets. At the time there were many pre-war copies of the News Chronicle Wireless Constructors Encyclopedia, as well as weekly magazines such as *Practical Wireless*, edited by F J Camm. This publication, known perhaps unjustly as Camm's Comic, was the foundation of many a later career in electronics. In addition to many 'built from scratch' projects, there were many articles on converting government surplus radio equipment for civilian use, including a primitive television set made from a modified radar unit. Many a journey was made on the trolleybus to Edgware Road, Paddington, where government surplus stores such as Smiths, sold for a few shillings, wartime radio sets that collectors are now happy to pay hundreds of pounds for, assuming they can ever be found.

COLLECTIONS.

Young boys, like magpies love to collect things. From 1940 to 1950 these were restricted for the most part to things that cost nothing to collect, but may have had some value in playground currency for swapping. Such items included pieces of shrapnel, found on the roads after air raids. The swap value of these depended on the size of the piece - fuse caps were particularly valuable.

Bus tickets were also collected, and at the time these were taken from a little clip-board carried by the bus conductor. They carried details of the bus route, and the price of the fare, the higher-priced tickets being harder to find. Although there was a ticket disposal slot on the bus platform, many people threw their tickets away after leaving the bus and the pavement beside every bus stop was generally awash with tickets.

Collecting railway locomotive numbers was another popular pursuit, with some boys becoming very knowledgeable on the subject. A favourite vantage point was the footbridge over the railway, between Lyon Park Avenue and London Road. The main line from Euston ran through Wembley, and a passenger train would pass every few minutes, as well as goods traffic.

The publisher Ian Allen, offered a series of booklets on the four railway companies with every locomotive from each company listed. These were known as stock books and the numbers could be underlined or ticked off as seen or 'copped'. The more enthusiastic collectors would travel great distances in order to see rare locomotives.

In the days of steam you would always find at main line terminals, a group of schoolboys, who, having bought their penny platform ticket, gathered at the end of the platform where the engines stopped, talking to the engine crew hoping to be invited up on to the footplate. A more dangerous pastime would be sneaking into the engine sheds at Willesden LMS or Old Oak Common GWR, which were strictly out of bounds. Dodging the shed foreman during these clandestine visits was a skill that would serve them in later years during National Service, when it was applied to avoiding the Sgt Major on army camps.

These depots were a fairly short bike ride away from Wembley, and a successful sortie into the engine sheds would guarantee several more numbers ticked off in their stock books.

Cigarette cards were always popular, and one would strive to find a complete series, which might amount to fifty cards. This could take many weeks or even months of playground trading. Other related collectables included matchboxes and cigarette packets.

These could be found on the pavements around Wembley, the majority of people being litter-bugs at that time. Most of the common brands of cigarette packets were easy to find, but others were quite rare, such as *Passing Cloud*, or *Black Cat,* which generally only sold in the north of England. Tobacco tins were also collected, but these were harder to find than cigarette packets.

Other collectables at that time were butterflies, moths and wild birds' eggs. Although comparatively rare today, birds and butterflies of all kinds were very common in the forties, and the eggs and butterflies were actually available commercially to collectors. The relative rarity of these creatures today is probably less the fault of collectors than the widespread use of pesticides, and wanton destruction and removal of ancient hedgerows on farms, encouraged by the Ministry of Agriculture over the past fifty years.

Stamp collecting was an ever popular hobby, and most boys' magazines carried advertisements by stamp dealers for packets of mixed stamps for a relatively small sum.

Many of these mixed bags contained German stamps bearing the picture of Adolf Hitler, rarely seen today. Most boys dabbled with stamp collecting at one time or another, but very few took up the hobby seriously.

Glass marbles were always popular, both from the collector's point of view, and for games played in the school playgrounds. Marbles came in various sizes and colours, some of the more unusual ones dating to Victorian times. In recent years, some of these older marbles have become quite sought after by adult collectors and command extraordinary prices. In the USA today, there is still one company making glass marbles, having been in business for over one hundred years, producing nothing else.

There were a number of children's publications, including comics such as *Dandy, Beano, Radio Fun* and the *Boys Own Paper*, most of which dated back to the thirties and were often collected. . Each one produced an Annual every year around Christmas time, and many of these showed up under the tree or in stockings at that time. Comics from that period in good condition are quite valuable today.

A newcomer to the scene, which gained immediate popularity, was the *Eagle* comic, appearing in 1950 for the first time, edited by Marcus Morris. Its most popular character was Dan Dare, a space pilot of the future. While there were many science fantasy paperback books available, this was the first publication of its kind aimed specifically at children. The so-called Horror Comics imported from the USA at the time, were not primarily published for young readers, but rather for somewhat juvenile adults.

Lead and tin soldiers were also fairly common, and some boys built up quite an extensive collection. Lead was easier to find than tin at the time and the composition of the toys reflected this. These soldiers did not survive many play sessions without suffering some damage, and any found today can command high prices from collectors. In the USA, Tony recently attended an estate auction where two sets of ten English toy soldiers, in somewhat battered condition in their original boxes, sold for nearly two hundred dollars each.

Tony's father was a brass-moulder at London Transport, and was able to make aluminium moulds of little navy ships, and aeroplanes, including a Spitfire. Tony therefore learned at an early age, to cast lead models, using the living room fireplace as a furnace and a plumbers ladle to melt the lead. When the supply of scrap lead ran out, he experimented with molten aluminium and destroyed the mould.

Lead was not regarded as a serious public health problem at the time. It should be remembered that probably 90 percent of the houses in England at the time used lead pipes for the cold water system, and iron pipes for the hot water system, which were subject to rust and corrosion. Connections to the street water main were invariably lead. It was a common ingredient in paint, which was possibly the greatest threat to health, until the proliferation of volatile lead additives to motor fuels, starting in the mid fifties.

PASTIMES.

Ex American army Bivouac tents each affords cover for two people, Height three feet seven inches, Length seven foot nine inches, width six feet. Weight complete with poles and pegs nine pounds. One end permanently open, brand new 37/6d each

Saunders & Kaye, Harrow Road, Kensal Rise.

OUTDOOR PASTIMES.

Children of the forties and fifties tended to acquire a remarkable variety of interests and hobbies. Many of these pastimes were seasonal, such as fishing or butterfly collecting. For those inclined towards sports, there was summer cricket, or winter football, either as a player or a spectator. Followers of local football teams attended Saturday football matches regardless of the weather, and it was not felt necessary to carry a weapon to the match or indulge in acts of vandalism afterwards if one's team happened to lose. As the old newsreels attest, the star players in their baggy shorts were every bit as skilled at the game as modern day 'Stars', and having scored a goal they did not indulge in hugging and kissing other players in their team as is customary these days. Indeed, such behaviour is unlikely to have been appreciated by the spectators, and would have resulted in hoots of derision and catcalls from the crowd.

Likewise, cricket matches were conducted in a quiet dignified manner. The spectators would show their appreciation by quiet applause. Shouting, cheering, and the use of air horns would not have been tolerated.

For those not inclined towards field sports or running round in circles on a track, cycling was a popular summer pastime. The more gregarious riders would join clubs and go riding in a pack, but most riders would be seen in ones and twos along the relatively deserted country roads. Motor traffic was not a problem up to the late fifties.

One of our favourite bike destinations was Ruislip Lido. This is an artificial lake originally built as a feeder for the Grand Junction canal, and used as a popular recreational facility since 1930. Amongst its attractions, the Lido featured a miniature railway as well as boating, swimming and a refreshments stand. During the war, a short ride on the underground from Alperton to South Harrow, followed by a bus ride, clutching a couple of bread and jam sandwiches, with a Thermos of tea or a bottle of water added up to a whole day out for next to nothing. In fact it was the nearest thing to a trip to the seaside the average child could hope for during those stressful times.

Post war, when air travel was still a novelty, a trip to Northolt Aerodrome was an inexpensive treat. The ex fighter field, still shared with the RAF, was where British European Airlines ran a Dakota service to various short haul destinations. The sprawling Heathrow airport was then still only a future nightmare.

The Dakota or DC3 was standard airline equipment until the British aircraft industry was geared up for post war production. It was one of the most reliable and versatile aircraft ever produced, and after nearly seventy years, there are still many of these old veterans flying, some in America still in passenger service.

Recently however, a number of "safety" regulations, promulgated by E.U. bureaucrats, will effectively end pleasure flights in the UK on any vintage aircraft capable of carrying more than fifteen passengers. Air Atlantique in Coventry had three of these aircraft for charter. Duxford and other museum airfields in England will also be affected by this stupidity. The requirements included safety escape chutes for the DC3, an aircraft with a cabin door only four feet above the ground and drop down oxygen masks in an aircraft which was not pressurized with a service ceiling below ten thousand feet, as well as bullet-proof doors to the pilot's compartment, and up to date radar and electronics. The cost of these modifications, even if one could go along with the manifest absurdity of the proposals, would amount to more than the original production cost of the aircraft, which would then, in any case, no longer be an unmodified vintage machine.

When these were flying from Northolt in the late forties, for sixpence, one could gain entrance to the observation area to watch the aircraft taking off and landing. For an extra threepenny bit, you were allowed to enter an out-of-service aircraft, and sit at the controls in the pilot's seat for a few minutes.

In addition to the commercial airliners, there was a De Haviland Dragon

Rapide, one of the prettiest biplane airliners ever built, making trips around London for fifteen shillings, a sum of money, which might just as well have been fifteen thousand pounds to a schoolboy in 1948. The aircraft would fly over Barham School and we would gaze out of the window dreaming of one day flying in it.

We did finally fly in such a machine at Duxford in 2006, for eighty-five pounds each, which in terms of real value was still close to the 1948 price, allowing for inflation. The Duxford trip however, was of much shorter duration than those around London.

CAMPING.

Camping was another popular pastime for people of modest incomes shortly after the war, and anybody considering this form of holiday in the late forties was faced with a vast choice of government surplus camping equipment flooding the market. Anything from small portable cooking stoves burning solid fuel tablets to full size field service cookers, two man pup tents, to large mess tents, water containers, hurricane and Tilley lamps, ground sheets, blankets, sleeping bags etc. The only problem to a person considering camping was the weight of all this equipment. Unless the would-be camper owned a car, the load had to be carried on his bicycle or on his back. On one memorable camping trip to a site near Lewes, Derek had a light-alloy rear carrier collapse under the weight of his camping gear, and had to purchase and fit a more robust, steel carrier before we could continue on our way, finally arriving at the site to pitch our pup tent in the darkness after midnight.

Groups of campers such as Boy Scouts might carry all their equipment in a two-wheel cart, but unless they made part of their journey by train, with the cart in the guards van, they were somewhat limited as to the distance they could cover.

Perhaps because there was less canned entertainment as a distraction, young people were more inclined to join various youth organizations such as the Boy Scouts and Guides, the various service groups such as the Sea Scouts, Air Training Corps, and Army cadets. There was also the Boys Brigade. We were both members of the latter organization.

In 1948 Capt. Frank Strange, who lived in Eagle Road, ably assisted by Officers Piper, Burgin, and A.N. Other, recruited boys from Wembley County, and Alperton School, to form the 1st Wembley Boys Brigade company, based at the Baptist church opposite Alperton School. Many recruits promptly deserted the various churches in the area, to sign on as Baptists, discovering that the more informal attitude of the Minister, Rev. Peck made his services far less bum-fidgety. In his younger days, Rev. Peck had been an enthusiastic constructor of wireless sets, and when he heard of Tony's interest in radio, we were privileged to be shown, in a small storeroom at the church, a television set, based on the Baird rotating disc system, which he had built in the early thirties. He sadly confessed that it had never worked. It is sad to relate that the good vicar passed away in May 2009 at the ripe old age of 97, and was still on occasions preaching up to the age of 93. Captain Strange and his officers were good men who devoted their time to the best interests of all the boys. The summer camps at Whitecliff Bay, on the Isle of Wight and at Bridport in Dorset, as well as the annual BB big show at the Albert Hall will be fondly remembered.

First Wembley Boys Brigade 1948, new recruit Tony awaits delivery of his uniform.

Derek was the more enthusiastic of the authors, and actually rose to the rank of corporal. Tony was the first to leave the group, never having been able to muster sufficient enthusiasm for marching up and down in a church hall, or the relatively heavy religious aspects of the organization.

DANCING.

In the days during and after the war, ballroom dancing was a popular pursuit, more so with girls who actually seemed to like dancing, than with boys who normally only went to a dance hall in order to meet girls. The usual scene at small dancehalls would have the boys sitting or lined up against one wall, the girls lined up against the opposite wall, with perhaps a few pairs of girls dancing together, and the occasional but rare boy and girl dancing.

For serious dance enthusiasts there was a ballroom attached to the Majestic cinema in Wembley High Street, and there were also dances held in the Town Hall. One of the largest dancehalls in the general area was the Hammersmith Palais. A chain of dance schools such as Guy Hayward's would generally be found above Burtons Men's Tailors shops. This would be as an alternative to a Billiard Hall chain, which also seemed to share a close relationship with Burtons.

These dance halls would die out as Rock & Roll took hold of the imagination of the younger generation, but prancing around with a vacant facial expression took the place of dancing in many public-house Jazz clubs. Such jazz venues in Wembley included the Hop Bine in North Wembley, and the Fox & Goose in Hangar Lane.

FISHING.

A more leisurely pursuit was fishing. Starting as small boys fishing with a net for sticklebacks, or newts, one progressed with age to a cheap fishing rod and reel along the canal bank. There was little to be caught in the canal at that time, but a short ride on the Underground would bring one to Uxbridge, for the river Colne, or a bus journey to the Thames. This was in the days before every inch of waterfront in the UK was claimed as the exclusive domain of various fishing clubs. Today very few places are accessible to non club members.

Fishing for sticklebacks normally led to the establishment of an aquarium or garden pond.

This could prove to be an expensive business for a boy with only a couple of shillings pocket money to spend. Even the smallest aquarium tank cost more than ten shillings at the time. As for garden ponds, an old kitchen sink would normally be pressed into service by those boys fortunate enough to find one. The sinks were stocked with whatever pond life the owner could catch, including pondweed, water snails, tadpoles, small fish, and newts. There was a seed merchants shop in Ealing Road next to Bowrons Avenue, which also stocked aquarium supplies, including small goldfish, and American catfish, which were available for a few pennies each. A number of these little catfish found their way into various rivers around the country and grew to monstrous sizes.

RECREATION

PARKS & OPEN SPACES.

Sudbury Park, the gift to Wembley, of the late Mr G. Titus Barham.

Wembley official guide, 1939

Wembley is well supplied with parks and open spaces, and our earliest recollections are of visits to the paddling pool at King Edward's Park, and attending the annual visit of the circus and fun fair at Barham Park. At least up until the early fifties, children could be left to play in these parks without adult supervision. There was generally a full time park keeper in attendance to keep an eye on things, and eject those young visitors who committed cardinal sins such as riding bicycles on the footpaths, littering, or fishing in the ornamental ponds. More serious offenders would be reported to the police.

BARHAM PARK

Barham Park, first named Sudbury Lodge, was built originally for the Copland sisters. Later it became the residence of the Barham family. Titus Barham, son of the founder of the Express Dairy Sir George Barham, upon his death in 1937 left the building, grounds and museum collection to the citizens of Wembley. Sadly neglected by the Wembley Council, during the war, it was used by various civil defence organizations. Derek remembers suffering from a nose bleed whilst playing in the park, and being enthusiastically dragged into the building by young Red Cross girls who administered various treatments to stop the bleeding.

Having been allowed to deteriorate for over twenty years, the building was torn down by the council in the 1950s causing a public outcry. A similar act of vandalism was perpetrated during the war when another fine building gifted to the council, Oakington Manor Farm was blown up as an ARP exercise.

On summer Saturday evenings towards the end of the war open air dances were held in front of the house for a short time. A five or six piece band provided the music. Watching and listening to these musicians had a strong influence on Derek, who later would himself become a band leader.

During the war the park was a meeting place for courting couples and many a carnal deed was committed after dark under an army greatcoat in the meadow. Each morning, it was part of the duty of the elderly park keeper to remove the offensive evidence of these liaisons

For any children growing up in Wembley, Barham Park was an irresistible attraction. In the early 40s there were still cows grazing in the large meadow behind the house. At that time the house had not yet been allowed to fall into a state of terminal decay by Wembley Council, and at least during the early part of the war there was a light aeroplane parked on the terrace at the side of the house facing the formal gardens. Our recollections of it are divided. Derek remembers a low wing monoplane, such as a Miles Magister while Tony recalls it as a high wing monoplane similar to an Auster. One thing we are agreed on is that it was finished in bright yellow paint, which was customary for training machines in the RAF. In retrospect, it seems likely that either of the relatively modern types mentioned would have been requisitioned for use in the armed forces, so it was probably an older model sports plane used for flying training in the thirties.

On the other side of the house there were a number of iron animal cages, which in past times may have held monkeys or other small animals. These cages were later joined by bomb casings, used by the ARP and Civil Defence workers for training purposes.

The park was at that time separated from the Harrow Road by a tall plank fence, and entry could only be made through the upper or lower gates.

The area from this fence to a point roughly half way to the park's drive, was heavily wooded with a variety of mature trees. Hidden in this wood, near the upper gate, was a little cottage surrounded by its own tall fence. This had probably been at one time a gatekeeper's lodge, and was reputed by the children at Barham School to have a madman living in it.

Tony out of curiosity one day looked through a knot hole in the fence and saw a boy with Downs syndrome, of about ten years of age playing with a ball. This poor child had the good fortune to be looked after by loving parents, rather than being consigned to a home for such unfortunates as would normally have been the case at that time. None the less, such was the ignorance of the times that Tony didn't stop running till he reached the park gates at the old Court.

Post war, every year would see a visit from Billy Smarts Circus. This was one of the largest travelling circuses with just about every animal circus act and routine known at the time. Billy Smart, always wearing a White Stetson hat, was a cigar chomping, larger-than-life character. Prior to the arrival of the circus he would show up at Phelps Publicity at Wembley Triangle to arrange for posters, bill-posting, and publicity. These meetings with Arthur Phelps would inevitably degenerate into a loud argument and shouting-match, much to the entertainment of the staff. Eventually a price would be agreed and both parties would retire to the Greyhound pub the best of friends, and each thinking he had got the best of the bargain.

Another annual event at the park was the fun-fair, again a very large collection of rides and shows including a Wall of Death and every other popular ride of the time. A Boxing Booth offered ten pounds to any local lad who felt he could go two rounds with the resident Pug. Those who felt lucky would entertain the crowd for the first round, and invariably find themselves on their back, midway through the second round. The .22 rifle range was always popular, and at that time there were still a few freak shows. These fairs in the mid fifties were a bedlam of different noises, from the siren on the bumper cars, to the strident organ on the large roundabout and the recorded music played on some of the other rides. The fairground was one of the only places a teenager could hear pop music played very loud. This provided the authors' first experience of Bill Haley, Freddy Bell & the Bell Boys, etc. This type of music was not customarily played by the BBC at the time.

An attraction which to us was equal to that of the fair itself was to view the huge Scammell and AEC road tractors which as well as hauling the fun-fair trailers around the country, would double up as generators to provide power for the lights and rides. These massive machines, radiating waves of heat with engines roaring were fascinating to young boys.

Most of them were of angular pre-war construction, modified for their present employment and painted in the colourful style favoured by showmen the world over. Lovingly maintained, they were kept spotlessly clean, with every brass fitting highly polished.

Today, the venue for the funfair is in the field between the railway embankment and Harrow Road in Sudbury. Whereas entry used to be free, people are now expected to pay for entry as well as for the rides.

Another event after the war remembered by Tony was a speech made by Winston Churchill at an open air meeting in the meadow beside the house, to drum up support for the Conservative candidate after the first four years of Labour rule.

The northern boundary of the park was the railway embankment, protected by a low wooden bar fence. This acted as a barrier to cattle, but not to young boys from Barham School, some of whom lived in the houses backing up to the other side of the railway.

Tony narrowly escaped being run over by a train crossing these tracks, having waited for a train in one direction to pass, ran across the tracks without realizing that another train was approaching in the opposite direction. The lesson was well learned.

At the Sudbury end of Barham Park is Barham Old Court, a collection of single story buildings arranged around an ornamental garden, the centrepiece of which was a wishing-well. At the front of the building inside the original lower gate was a courtyard dominated by a large mulberry tree.

In 1952 a public library was opened in the Old Court, and later in 1956 a youth club was opened, in which Derek would rehearse his Jazz band.

Parts of the old park ornamental gardens still exist, but sadly are only a ghost of the beautifully maintained grape arbour and flower beds of the forties and fifties.

KING EDWARD VII PARK

King Edward VII Park in the centre of Wembley had 26 acres of open space, with paved footpaths, a bandstand and a large paddling pool for children.

There was a small refreshment kiosk next to the pool. Other attractions included six grass tennis courts and four hard courts, and a bowling green. The pool was drained during the war and never reopened after hostilities had ended. It is possible that the polio scare after WW2 had a bearing on the decision to close the pool. All that now remains is a circular footpath defining its shape. The bandstand also vanished during the war, possibly a victim of the scrap metal drive in 1940.

There were two entrances to the park in Park Lane, and one by a footpath leading to St Johns Road.

A large area of the park now laid out for football pitches, was ploughed up during WW2 for allotment gardens.

ONE TREE HILL.

One Tree Hill is described in the Wembley Directory as a park of some twenty acres, with a good elevation commanding a fine view of the surrounding country. It goes on to claim that Windsor Castle can be clearly seen in the distance. We have to take this claim on trust. Growing up in the area, we can rarely recall when Horsenden Hill was clearly visible through the smog and industrial haze. Windsor Castle would never have been visible.

The park is bounded on one side by the Piccadilly line railway embankment, and the various streets bordering Ealing Road on the other. At the narrowest point, there is a convenient footpath providing a shortcut from the end of Bowrons Avenue, passing under the railway to the Bridgewater Road. From the end of Bowrons Avenue two smaller footpaths lead over the top of the hill, one of them leading to Braemar Avenue, and the other leading to St James's Gardens. A further path leads over the back of the hill, passing One Tree Hill children's clinic before arriving at a second footway under the railway, a short distance from the bus garage.

At one time there was an impressive stand of elm trees on the top of the Hill, and another avenue of giant elm trees towards the end of Farm Avenue. These were destroyed by Dutch Elm disease, and were never replanted.

Our earliest memories of the park revolve around the children's playground which contained swings, both for infants and for larger children, a roundabout, two see-saws, a slide and a maypole. These playground items were removed for scrap during the war. All that remained was the maypole with one solitary short chain attached, which when blown against the pole by the wind produced a sad and distinctive ringing sound, and the central hub of the roundabout, which still rotated, and could be ridden on, by standing on the short brackets at its base and clinging to the steel ball at the top. The playground was restored after the war, and provided a great deal of enjoyment to the local children for many years. There is no sign of it today, for whatever reason

Before the war, there was a small kiosk selling snacks and ice cream at the top of the hill. During the war, the entire area was ploughed up and turned into allotment gardens.

BARN HILL.

Barn Hill Park, located at the north end of Wembley near the Town Hall. It also commands a wonderful view, having an elevation of 300 feet. The top of the hill was covered by an impressive stand of beech trees, and there are several dew ponds, which when first seen by Tony were teeming with minnows.

Our first visit to the park was around 1950 when we had our first bicycles. Barn Hill was a little too far out of the way to have been visited on foot and we hardly knew of its existence.

The park was apparently the original site of the Wembley Golf Club, although we cannot recall any sign of it. The back side of the hill ran down into farm land which was still being worked up to the sixties. The farm land continued on the other side of Fryent Way, and is now apparently a part of Fryent Country Park. The west side of the farm land is bounded by the underground railway line to Kingsbury

THE LMS SPORTS FIELDS.

While not strictly speaking a public open space, this area, extends from the buildings fronting the Harrow Road, formally Simpsons American car dealership, as far as the LMS railway tracks, at the bottom of London Road. There is a public footpath running alongside the sports ground, connecting with the Harrow Road and London Road, continuing by way of a footbridge over the railway to Lyon Park Avenue.

In addition to the sports facilities, there was a wooden club house where occasionally dances and other LMS social gatherings would take place

At the bottom of the sports field, adjacent to the railway, was the siding where coal for the London Passenger Transport Board power station was unloaded. The power station, notable for its wartime camouflage murals of houses and trees on the old cooling towers and chimneys, is long gone.

The Wembley Brook runs alongside the railway embankment on its way to join the Brent alongside Stonebridge Park tube station.

As was the case with most other park spaces, much of this area was given over to allotment gardens during, and for some time after the war.

ALPERTON AREA.

One Tree Hill Park, already described, extends well into the area of Alperton, and the largest area of open space other than this is the Alperton Sports Field, on Alperton Lane. Bounded by Manor Farm Road, Burns Road, Alperton Lane and the Manor Farm factory estate. This area offers a number of facilities to the public, including two football pitches, a running track and a number of tennis courts. Our memories of the place are less than pleasant, having endured many a cold and foggy winters' day there during our school days. The public refuse incinerator has now been replaced by factories, so the air is no doubt a good deal less toxic than in those halcyon days.

Another less known little park in Alperton is the children's playground, situated on Mount Pleasant, near the intersection with Woodstock Road. This is a very small area, of about an acre, mainly grassed over, but with a little play area of swings and roundabouts.

SUDBURY AREA.

Sudbury contains a wealth of open spaces, the largest of which is Horsenden Hill, covering 228 acres, and extending into Perivale. During our schooldays there was still a working farm at the canal end of the park, which also shared a border with the Sudbury Golf Club, whose links extended from the Bridgewater Road down to the canal, bordering on the aforementioned farm. Today, the farm appears to have been absorbed by the golf club. The boundary between the private golf club and the park started around the Ashness Gardens entrance, and consisted of an old unpaved lane, with an avenue of trees, extending all the way to the canal bridge at Horsenden Lane, which defined the western boundary of the park. On the other side of the lane, was another working farm, and the ruins of a little house, known to children as the Chinese house. The whole area of the ruin was overgrown, and only the foundations of the old house remained. Horsenden Lane extends around the park, passing the Ballot Box public house, finally ending in the Whitton Avenue housing estate. There is still open land extending from the west side of Horsenden Lane, all the way to the Greenford Road

On the Ashness Gardens end of the park was a small nine hole public golf course, extending up to the summit on the east side of the hill.

During the early fifties, the entire north side of the Hill was excavated and a large underground reservoir was constructed, as part of the government's optimistic civil defence precautions against atomic attack. There it remains, although there is very little sign of it today above ground. However, the square outline of the reservoir can be clearly defined on Google satellite photographs.

It is now possible on a clear day to see the Crystal Palace TV mast from the top of the hill, a feat that only became possible after the implementation of the Clean Air Act of 1956. Previous to this, the entire London basin would be almost continuously filled by industrial haze and smog.

At the point where the Harrow Road forks into the Watford Road, at the end of the 662 trolleybus route, is a small triangular patch known as Butlers Green, amounting to possibly two acres, containing a children's play area with a slide and swings. At the opposite end of this little park, by the Swan public house, was a public convenience, now boarded up, no doubt as an economy measure, implemented by the council without regard to the needs of the public.

Across the Watford Road from Butlers Green is the entrance to the Vale Farm sports area, home in the forties and fifties of the Vale Farm outside swimming pool, and the Wembley Wasps Rugby team. Since those days the sports facility has been greatly expanded to include a running track and other features and appears to have expanded up to East Lane.

Hidden away between Sudbury Court Road, and the Watford and Harrow Roads, is Elmwood Park, a small green area with mature trees. It is a pleasant spot to walk the dog, and relatively unknown other than to those living in the area. It has the distinction of retaining a small area still given over to wartime allotment gardens, which for over sixty years have been enthusiastically maintained by their owners.

WEMBLEY WATERWAYS.

Messing about in boats.

Water has always powerfully attracted young boys, and we were no exception to the rule. As pupils of Barham School one of our favourite pastimes was catching newts in the large pool which existed at the bottom of the water garden cascade at Barham Park. Alas the old pool has long since gone, although a few of the little cascade pools still exist partially choked with litter. The newts would only appear in the spring when they took to the water to breed. At other times, sticklebacks could be caught from the forbidden towpath of the canal at Alperton. The sight of a small boy in short trousers wearing a school cap, carrying a jam-jar with a string handle, and a home made fishing net, was a common sight in the forties. In fact, jam-jars were very hard to find at that time, since most were re-used by housewives making home-made jam and pickles, or collected for salvage. Some boys managed to get hold of an old kitchen sink to use as a makeshift garden pond, and hours were spent watching the activities of the aquatic life they had collected.

As time passed the move to Alperton School, and the acquisition of bicycles made it possible to visit places such as the ponds behind the Empire Pool, on the old exhibition site. Even the Welsh Harp reservoir, and the Stanmore Ponds were within a half hours ride.

The back side of the dam on the Welsh Harp could be reached by an alleyway behind the houses on Birchan Grove, off Blackbird Hill. After heavy rains, with the Brent in flood, it was a spectacular sight.

Later, the purchase of an ex-RAF type K, one man rubber dinghy from Saunders & Kaye, an army surplus store situated on the Harrow Road in Kensal Rise, opened new horizons. As the dinghies were sold without a pump they had to be inflated by lung power, a job that always left the would-be navigator hyper-ventilated and dizzy. The sheet rubber floor of the dinghy always seemed to contain small holes that could never be found, but which always seemed to leave the occupant sitting in a puddle of water. However, deflated, these treasures would fit easily on the rear carrier of a bicycle. Several crossings of the small spur of the Welsh Harp were made, many years before it became the exclusive domain of a sailing club.

PONDS AROUND WEMBLEY.

Before they had been allowed to degenerate into their present relatively dilapidated condition, the gardens of the old Barham Hall were beautifully laid out. The two semi-circular ornamental ponds, on the main walkway to the house contained goldfish in the forties, but are now choked with reeds. Farther over, there was a smaller pathway through a grape arbour which led to a water garden, consisting of a cascade of small pools and miniature waterfalls, which led down to a large pond, about 50 feet by 20. The paved path led along one side of this pond, which in springtime attracted a variety of amphibians. The newts and tadpoles became the quarry of many young boys who were prepared to risk a confrontation with the park keeper.

There was also a large pond in the back garden of the large house serving as a nurses' home, situated on the Harrow Road next to the park entrance opposite Linthorpe Avenue. Neither of these two ponds contained small fish, so their attraction was purely seasonal.

It should be mentioned that access to the pond in the garden of the nurses' home involved climbing a fence from the park and trespassing on private property.

When bicycles became available several more ponds were discovered in the area around Wembley. The top of Barn Hill contains two good sized ponds which were teeming with minnows when first seen in the fifties.

There was another pond at Kennedy's Farm in Alperton, partially filled with rubbish. It was accessible from One Tree Hill Park, beside Alperton station. This area is now part of the new Alperton School.

Finally there was a good sized farm pond off Horsenden Lane, near the Ballot Box pub. At the time this was still a working farm, and small boys were not welcome.

Still further from Wembley, but accessible by bicycle was the big pond at Gunnersbury Park in Ealing. This offered small rowing boats for hire for a modest sum, and was the destination for many an evening bike ride.

WEMBLEY RIVERS.

The river Brent, which has given its name to the borough of which Wembley is a part, was at one time, before the area was built up, a clean and healthy river. It probably contained trout, and was certainly clean enough for the local children to swim in. The river had been dammed at Hendon to provide a feeder for the Grand Junction canal, and a sizable lake known as the Welsh Harp was formed, named after a prominent public house on its banks. Probably a third of the river's flow is diverted to the canal, so the section passing through Wembley would originally have been much deeper than it is today. Shortly after leaving the dam, the Brent crosses Neasden Lane at the bottom of Blackbird Hill, and continues on through the area now occupied by the Wembley Stadium and the adjacent trading estate. At some point in this area, it is joined by the Wealdstone

Brook. Up to the fifties, this was a swampy location, extending as far as the Harrow Road at Stonebridge. Today there appears to be a green area between Monks Park, and the council estates bordering the North Circular Road. From this point, the Brent was fed through a concrete channel and occasional tunnels, passing behind the Ace Café, under the Grand Junction Canal through an old red brick viaduct, and continuing on to cross the Hangar Lane beside Alperton Lane. After crossing the road, the river was allowed to flow in its original bed, past the municipal dump before crossing the Western Avenue a short distance to the east of Alperton Lane, entering Ealing.

Even today the Brent is a dead river, although the source of pollution is less obvious than in the past. The original major source of pollution was the British Oxygen factory at Hendon, which dumped thousands of tons of Calcium Carbide, used in the manufacture of Acetylene gas, on the banks of the Welsh Harp. Over the years the lake recovered, and has now been restocked with a variety of fish. The Brent however, as observed from the back of the Ace Café, still only contains grey slime instead of the green algae to be expected in a healthy river. In the past it was customary for factories to dump their filth into the nearest stream, and the seepage from the huge dumps alongside the river at Stonebridge, and Alperton Lane must have contributed to the general pollution. With today's more stringent controls, it can be hoped that one day the Brent will once again be home to more than leeches and bacteria.

There are two other streams running through Wembley. The larger of these, originally known as the Wealdstone Brook, is in Wembley Park, crossing under Empire Way at Wembley Park railway station, and flowing alongside Olympic Way into the old trading estate, finally joining the River Brent in what used to be the swampy undeveloped triangular area, bounded by railways, but is now built over with factories and supermarkets having direct access to the North Circular Road.

The smaller stream, known as the Wembley Brook was far more interesting, as it was open and available to young boys for a variety of interesting pursuits. Unfortunately, like all local rivers at the time it was polluted to the point where only a grey slime and small leeches could live in it. Even sticklebacks, which are notable for their ability to tolerate polluted water were absent from this little stream. Its source was uncertain, but it probably originated somewhere in Kenton.

The original route of this brook seems to have been alongside the LMS tracks from North Wembley, curving under Lancelot Road, crossing under Wembley High Street, and emerging behind the shops on the right hand side of the Ealing Road. Access to the stream was either by the flight of steps opposite the Railway Hotel, or from Chaplin Road. It then crossed under Chaplin Road in a brick culvert, which collapsed in 1948 and was replaced by a larger concrete channel, continuing in the open until it crossed under the Ealing Road, emerging behind Coronet Parade. It then continued along behind the houses in Lyon Park Avenue, past the old allotment gardens on the railway embankment, crossing under the railway through a fine brick tunnel, near the point where the footbridge crosses the railway from Lyon Park Avenue to London Road. Finally, running between the railway sidings for the power station, and the LMS sports field, it found its way into the Brent somewhere near the Stonebridge Park railway station.

Derek recalls sometime in 1947, watching Italian POW workers constructing a concrete culvert for the brook where it passed under the LNER Railway embankment in Lancelot Road.

Today, the little stream has been entirely enclosed as it passes through the Wembley business district, and exists only in the memories of those who grew up in the area.

THE GRAND JUNCTION CANAL.

Originally completed in 1801, the Grand Junction Canal passes through Wembley from Perivale at Horsenden Lane, to the aqueduct across the North Circular Road at Park Royal.

After passing through Greenford, the canal connects to the Grand Union Canal at Hanwell, and after being joined by the river Brent passes into the Thames through a tidal lock near Hampton Court.

In the other direction the canal turned east leaving Wembley, and continued on through Paddington and the Islington tunnel, connecting with the River Lea, and the docks at Limehouse. Today the area has been claimed by property developers for yuppie accommodation, but in the forties, the canal provided a rear view of some of the worst slums and bomb damaged properties that London had to offer.

In Wembley, the Ealing Road crossed the canal by a modern concrete bridge opposite the Alperton Bus garage.

At the bridge, on each side of the road, a rough track ran down to the canal towpath, providing access for boys fishing for sticklebacks, which were one of the few life forms able to tolerate the oily polluted water. The occasional serious angler might be seen, whose optimism was not yet blunted by experience. The best he could hope for were a few stunted roach, and the occasional gudgeon. Despite warnings to stay away from the canal, with threats of corporal punishment, the towpath was an irresistible magnet for schoolboys of all ages. On the towpath side of the canal at the Alperton Bridge was a glass works with a mountain of broken bottles in its yard. The factory possessed an enormous single cylinder gas engine, with a flywheel fully fifteen feet in diameter. Watching this monster huffing and puffing was a favourite pastime for boys passing by.

After the war, the availability of ex-RAF type K rubber dinghies added a new dimension of enjoyment, if not danger to older boys who would paddle their leaking craft across to the opposite bank bordering the golf links, looking for lost golf balls in the water. There were also areas where interesting Victorian bottles and jars could be 'mined' from the bank at the site of old rubbish dumps.

After dark, the towpath and the underside of the bridges at Ealing Road and Manor Farm Road, became the meeting place for degenerates and perverts of the worst description. Messages, inviting participation in lewd behaviour were often to be found chalked on the walls under the bridges. It is rumoured that this area is still a popular venue for such liaisons.

In the late forties, the canal still carried a fair amount of commercial traffic, and pleasure craft were relatively rare. Much of the cargo consisted of timber and there were a number of timber yards alongside the waterway. In the Wembley area, one of these was beside the bridge at Horsenden Lane, and another was at Alperton beside the underground railway viaduct.

Many of the narrow-boats were still horse-drawn in the forties, but more and more were eventually powered by single cylinder 'thumper' engines, such as those manufactured by Petter, Beardmore and Lister. These would often be seen towing one or more un-powered craft.

Huge municipal dumps were commonly found along the Grand Junction banks, which leached toxins into the water, and any person having the misfortune to fall into the canal in these areas was well advised to have his stomach pumped out in the nearest hospital.

During WW2, the IRA attempted to blow up the aqueduct crossing the North Circular Road, a short distance from Hangar Lane. Despite their best efforts, little damage was done, and wartime barge traffic went on unabated. A short distance from the North Circular Road is the old brick viaduct, which carries the canal over the river Brent. It is possible to speculate that the same amount of Gelignite used on the concrete viaduct might have successfully brought down this old structure, causing an equal amount of disruption to the transport system.

A short distance along the towpath from the Alperton Bridge was a footbridge linking Beresford Avenue and Carlyon Road. Sometime in the early fifties, this section of the canal was drained for repairs and cleaning. As many as fifty old bicycle frames, together with a mass of other rubbish like old prams and even gas stoves which had been thrown off the footbridge became visible as the water receded.

Today there is little if any commercial traffic, and the majority of craft found on the canal are pleasure boats, together with a large number of converted or purpose built narrow-boats used by holiday makers or in many cases as homes by the owners.

It must also be admitted that the water is fairly clean these days, and a large variety of good-sized fish can be found in areas which were virtually dead in past days.

Up until the war a daily passenger boat operated from Paddington to Greenford with passengers who could have lunch on board.

WEMBLEY STADIUM AND EMPIRE POOL AND ARENA.

The Empire's greatest centre of sport.

The architects for the stadium and exhibition grounds were Sir John Simpson, and Maxwell Ayton, and the main construction contractor was Robert McAlpine.

Wembley stadium was built at a cost of 750,000 Pounds, requiring twenty five thousand tons of concrete, one thousand five hundred tons of construction steel, and a half million rivets. Work was completed in 300 working days, in time for the 1923 FA cup final in which Bolton Wanderers beat West Ham United, 2-0, after a delayed start due to crowds swarming on to the pitch.

The stadium was a part of the major development of Wembley Park for the 1924 Empire Exhibition. It was constructed on the site of the failed Wembley Tower, known as Watkins Folly, which never rose above its first stage, and was demolished in 1907

The stadium was one of the first large buildings to be built completely of reinforced concrete, leading edge technology at the time. Even after completion there were doubts in some quarters as to the strength of the structure. In order to put these doubts to rest, a battalion of guardsmen were ordered to mark time in the stands. The test was successful and the soldiers escaped unscathed.

In 1924, the British Empire Exhibition opened to become the Mecca for hundreds of thousands of visitors during that year and the next.

In December 1927, the stadium was opened for Greyhound racing, followed by Speedway racing in 1929. In the early days, a few female speedway riders were featured but proved to be unpopular and were discontinued. In 1929 the stadium also hosted the first Rugby League final.

In 1948 the stadium hosted the Olympic Games, and for a short time Wembley enjoyed worldwide fame. Under managing director Arthur Elvin's guidance Wembley stadium and pool became two of the major sporting venues in Europe.

There is a certain irony in the fact that although providing the venue for cup finals and international football matches, Wembley had no football team of its own. There was however, a first class dirt track Speedway team, and this, together with greyhound racing provided regular evening entertainment for the townspeople before television reduced the attendance to an uneconomical level.

The international football and Rugby League matches, and cup finals were generally held on weekends, and as a rule, many more supporters than the stadium could accommodate would show up in Wembley. This often resulted in a flood of supporters, who, being without tickets, and having missed the match, would appear in the shopping areas of the high street, often wearing kilts, and hopelessly intoxicated, reeling from one side of the pavement to the other, their mood being either happy or belligerent depending upon whether Scotland had won or lost the match.

The cup final and international football matches were ticket holder only events and often, supporters without tickets would offer large cash bribes to the turnstile operators in an effort to gain entry. For this reason the stadium management tried to recruit trustworthy casual workers, many of whom were off duty policemen and firemen from Wembley and Kingsbury. For routine Speedway and greyhound racing events the price of entry started from two shillings including program.

During the war, the troops evacuated from Dunkirk were taken to the stadium, which served as an emergency dispersal centre. When the last soldier had left the stadium, it became, together with the Empire Pool, a temporary shelter for hundreds of refugees from France, Belgium and Holland, until more permanent accommodation could be found for them.

Later in the war, military tattoos and Home Guard parades were held at the stadium. In addition to the wartime FA cup finals, daytime greyhound racing was introduced.

The old stadium was demolished in 2000, and a classic example of architecture gone mad was reopened in 2007. If a plebiscite had been held to determine whether the old building should be retained or destroyed, it would surely still be standing. It was pointed out that the two old towers could have been incorporated into the new building, requiring only a good coat of new paint and a good scrubbing with Jeyes Fluid disinfectant but to no avail. The present eyesore will doubtless remain until the opportunity arises for vested interests to make a great deal of money by replacing it on some pretext, when, it too, in its turn, will be demolished, possibly to be replaced by an even more absurd structure.

The Empire Pool, built approximately ten years after the stadium, at a cost of around 200,000 pounds, was intended for the Empire Games in 1934.

The architect was Irwin Williams, who had been the site engineer on the stadium and exhibition grounds project. It was in its time the largest indoor swimming pool in England featuring a unique wave generating device, and after the swimming events in the Empire Games, a boxing ring was placed in the centre of the pool supported by 'straps'. The Pool was also used in the same way for the Olympic Games of 1948. After the Olympics, the pool was boarded over and the arena used for a variety of sporting events such as the annual six-day bicycle race, and regular exhibition basketball displays by the Harlem Globetrotters. It was also the venue for a three-ring circus, and the children attending Barham School at the time were taken to view this American innovation. To the young mind a three-ring circus made no sense, since there was too much going on at once to see everything, and half the performance was therefore missed.

Equipment had also been installed that enabled the arena to be used as an ice rink, and for almost three decades there were two ice hockey teams in Wembley, the Wembley Lions, and the Wembley Monarchs.

Canadians made up the Wembley Monarchs team, and the Wembley Lions were British players. Attendance dwindled, again as television kept people at home in the evenings, and the ice hockey was discontinued in the sixties. However, the popularity of the Empire Pool did not diminish, and the launch of 'Ice Pantomimes' in the fifties drew large audiences.

While sports events are still held in the arena, ranging from boxing matches to table tennis, from the seventies onwards, pop music events tended to dominate, and draw crowds beyond anything the designers of the original arena could imagine.

The name of the Empire Pool was changed to 'The Wembley Arena' after major refurbishment, shortly before the construction of the new Wembley Stadium.

It would be unfair to consider the history of the stadium and pool without mentioning the man who became the leading light in promoting these facilities. From selling cigarettes from a kiosk at the exhibition in 1923, Arthur Elvin was made an honorary freeman of the Borough of Wembley in 1943, an MBE in 1945, and was granted a knighthood in 1946. In 1947 following the death of Chairman Lord Mottistone, Elvin became chairman as well as managing director. He held this position until his death in 1957.

THE XIVth OLYMPIAD.

The important thing about the Olympics was not winning, but taking part. The essential thing in life is not conquering but fighting well.

Baron Pierre De Coubertin

In 1948, Wembley hosted the Olympic Games, the main venue being Wembley Stadium, and the Empire Pool. The whole area had once been the site of the Empire Exhibition of 1924. The Empire Pool had been built ten years later for the Empire Games.

After the 1936 Olympics in Germany, it was planned to hold the next games in Helsinki in 1940, and in Britain in 1944. Of course, the war intervened, and it was decided that the first post war games of 1948 should be held in this country.

Known as the austerity games, the U.K. being at the time virtually bankrupt, it was out of the question to build new facilities for the Olympics, so a great effort was made to clean up the old site and make it presentable for visitors. Most of the old exhibition buildings had been requisitioned by the government

during the war and used for storage. For practical purposes they were now useless, with the exception of the Palace of Arts, which was used for the fencing events. The arts building was later taken over for several years by Tyresoles, a tyre remoulding company. Later still it became the base for the outside broadcast department of the BBC.

There was also an ice factory, which at best could be described as an eyesore, standing squarely in front of one approach to the stadium entrance.

None the less, the government pressed ahead, building the Olympic Way, a road running from the Wembley Park underground station to the entrance to the stadium. A subway was built running under Park Lane from the station to this new road.

German and Italian prisoners of war were pressed into service to assist in the construction. Derek recalls the Germans speaking very good English, and having money with which children would be rewarded for running little errands for them, but generally it was felt that the Germans were sullen compared to the Italians who were far more cheerful and outgoing.

After the games, a new pub known as 'The Torch' was built opposite the station, and as far as we know, remains the only relic of the Olympics other than the road.

Accommodation was found for the four thousand contestants locally, with some Wembley residents providing bed and breakfast. Other contestants were found accommodation at RAF Uxbridge, which was regarded as the Olympic village, and at RAF Stanmore. Also utilized, were ex military bases at Richmond Park and West Drayton as well as at certain area schools, including Wembley County, and other accommodation was secured in other venues, some far removed from Wembley

We reproduce below an abbreviated article from the Wembley County School magazine of the time:

It was only fitting that when the eyes of sportsmen everywhere were turned towards Wembley on the occasion of the XIV Olympics, that Wembley County School should be asked to provide accommodation for some of our visitors from overseas. After school broke up for the

summer holidays, Ministry of Works removal teams started on the task of transforming the school into a residential Hotel, with such addition in the way of training facilities as would naturally be required by competitors taking part in a world sporting contest…

Most of the classrooms upstairs became dormitories, each competitor had a comfortable bed, a bedside rug, and a half share in a wardrobe…. Downstairs there were three smaller dormitories, but most of the rooms were used for 'social' purposes.…

With the exception of the laboratories the assembly hall and the Headmasters room, all the downstairs rooms were used for one purpose or another, All had attractive curtains at the windows and most had coloured coconut matting on the floor. Perhaps the prettiest room of all was the dining room…

In keeping with the new function of the school, the entrance lobby was transformed into a hotel lounge…

The school not only served as a residential hotel for some fifty to sixty competitors, but was also a transport control centre and a training centre for boxing, wrestling, and, for the first week or so, weight lifting. For these latter purposes competitors of many countries came from numerous other centres to train in the gym …

We welcomed teams of college students who came to help on the reception and catering staffs. These cheerful people had to learn their job before starting on it, but in a surprisingly short time, with the help of our own kitchen staff and our domestic helpers under Mr Bonnet's skilful management, we were ready for the arrival of our guests.….. As each 'Nation' arrived they were welcomed by the Centre Commandant, and the Chef de Mission of the team was invited to break the national flag at the masthead…

Alperton School was not used, possibly because it was considered too Spartan for even the less affluent national teams. The reeking outside toilets and total lack of showers etc. may have influenced the decision.

At Barham School, which we were attending at the time, the Olympics became the focus of a frenzy of enthusiasm by teachers. Although the school would be closed for the summer holidays during the actual games, a great deal of class time was spent studying the history of the games, and the various athletic events.

The British contestants, unlike many other participants, received no help from the government, and had to provide all their own equipment and travel expenses. In many cases the time spent attending the games was set against the athletes annual holiday entitlement, and in at least two cases, contestants were sacked for attending. A major concession by the government was to raise their weekly ration of food to that of a manual labourer. After several years of wartime and post war food rationing, the British athletes were considerably less robust than most other nationalities.

The games opening ceremony took place on 29th July, before a crowd of 82,000, in a heat wave, with a recorded temperature of 93 degrees Farenheit. As might be expected in the UK, this was followed by a period of torrential rain lasting for two or three days.

The area's Boy Scouts were used to carry messages and release the seven thousand white doves of peace from around the track, as well as parading with the name boards in front of the participating nations.

A total of 59 nations participated in the 1948 games and there were 136 events many of them spread around various venues in the UK. These included cycling, rowing, equestrian events, fencing, Gymnastics, shooting, weight lifting, wrestling, and yacht racing. Outstanding athletes such as Emil Zatopek from Czechoslovakia, and Fanny Blankers-Koen, a housewife and mother from Holland, set new records.

The Empire pool was used for the last time as a swimming pool in the games, and nine new swimming records were set at this time. After the swimming events a boxing ring was installed above the pool for the boxing contests. Seventeen world and Olympic records were set at the stadium.

Over 1 million visitors passed through the turnstiles and six thousand competitors from the 59 nations participated.

The Olympics at this time were virtually un-politicized, even though Germany and Japan were excluded from the 1948 events. Italy however, was allowed to participate. Soviet Russia declined to attend.

A great deal was made of Baron de Coubertin's proposition that participation was more important than winning. This slogan was displayed on the scoreboard in the stadium. Looked at in the light of todays ultra competitive and nationalistic Olympics, the sentiment seems naïve to the point of absurdity.

Although the Berlin Games of 1936 had been partially televised for closed circuit viewing, this was to be the first occasion when all the stadium events were televised live, and a great many primitive and expensive TV sets were purchased by people who could ill afford them, providing a small, dim, flickering picture in a partially darkened room for a dozen or more neighbours who were invited round to watch the show. The coverage was limited to the London area, within range of the Alexandra Palace transmitter, but was still a benchmark television event.

At the end of the games on the 14th August the USA came top with 83 medals, 38 of which were gold. Sweden came second with 44 medals, including 16 gold, and France third with 29 medals including 10 gold. Unfortunately, not enjoying the large steaks the Americans had flown in daily, or the vast amounts of wine brought over by the French team, the half starved British team which had entered every event, only managed twelfth place with 23 medals, 3 being gold. Nevertheless in the cycling, at Herne Hill for the track racing, and road racing at Windsor Great Park, we won a medal in every event, 3 silvers and 2 bronzes.

Despite the financial constraints of the times, the games could be counted both as an international success, and from the government's point of view, a financial success. For the modest outlay of seven hundred and thirty thousand pounds, they were able to show a net profit of twenty thousand pounds, nine thousand of which was promptly demanded by the Inland Revenue.

BICYCLES.

It's strong, it's speedy, and it's smart in every way. The pride of any schoolboy's heart, it's time you had a BSA.

BSA Cycles advertisement in Boys Own Paper 1948

After the war, the commonest form of wheeled transport was the bicycle. Most workers would ride to and from work on a bike, and older children would ride to and from school. The alternative would be to walk, or if the journey was a long one, to travel by bus. The very idea of a school bus in Wembley would have been laughed at in those days.

The beneficial exercise provided by this mode of travel, combined with sugar and sweet rationing up to the 50s, kept most children down to a healthy weight.

Many of the bicycles in use by adults, were older pre-war heavy-frame machines with standard 'sit-up-and-beg' handlebars, and rod brakes. The larger models of these, with 28-inch-wheels were favoured by the police for patrols in country districts. The policeman's cape, still carried in some areas, would be folded over the handlebars.

There were relatively few cars on the road in the forties, so the police were able to pay more attention to cyclists, committing grave offences such as riding without lights after lighting-up time (published daily in the newspapers) or riding on the pavement or on park footpaths. These transgressions were prosecuted vigorously, as are petty motoring offences today.

Since batteries were expensive, most people avoided using their lights until it really got dark. Lighting-up time was usually in early twilight when visibility was quite good. The solution for those who were forced to ride after dark was to get a small dynamo which rested on the side of either the front or rear tyre. Some makes of tyres actually had a special tread on the side for the dynamo to work on. The dynamo was mounted on a spring pivot enabling it to be removed from the wheel when not needed. Later, in the early fifties, Raleigh machines were produced with a dynamo built into the front wheel hub, or combined with a three-or four-speed gear train in the rear wheel hub. These were for a time beyond the financial reach of most people. Incredibly, there were still a fair number of pre-war acetylene lamps in use, and tall tins of Calcium Carbide were still available from bicycle shops well into the fifties.

In addition to lights, bicycles were required to have a rear safety reflector, and a white patch of twelve square inches or more. This would normally be painted at the bottom of the rear mudguard. A warning bell was also mandatory.

At that time, bicycle frames were made with a crossbar for men or without a crossbar for ladies, who in those days would normally be wearing a dress. There were many different makes of bike available, most of which could be recognized by a distinctive front forks design, and a makers badge on the steering bracket below the handlebars.

Among the most common were Raleigh, Rudge, Phillips, Dayton, BSA, Royal Enfield, Triumph, Hercules, Armstrong and several others, now all long gone from the scene.

The old upright bikes were rejected by younger riders, in favour of the more modern sports bikes which were lighter in weight, with cable operated caliper brakes and 'drop' handlebars. The majority of the post war cycles produced in England used lightweight Reynolds 531 steel tubing, and there were countless bicycle shops where accessories could be purchased to personalize ones machine. One of the survivors from that period is Halfords, which had a shop in Wembley High Road between the police station and Ealing Road. At the time, Halfords was primarily a bicycle accessory shop, but over the years the company was able to adapt and change to car accessories and other lines of merchandise.

Other bicycle dealers failed to adapt to the changes over the years and went out of business. There were three bicycle shops in Ealing Road, Fruins and Alperton cycle works, situated midway down Ealing Road approximately opposite Eagle Road and Bowrons Avenue. The third shop was located at the junction of Chaplin Road. All of these shops closed as people turned away from bicycles in favour of cars in the late fifties.

Bob Keeler was an enterprising ex-motorcycle racer who managed to acquire Fruins and set up a used motorcycle shop. In the early days, many of the machines on offer were somewhat less than roadworthy, but the quality improved with business success. Derek acquired a Norton Dominator motorcycle from Bob Keeler in 1960 for 119 Pounds, which gave him excellent service. As the adjacent properties became vacant Bob Keeler took them over, expanding his business from motorcycles to used cars, and finally to a car hire business.

Tony was late in getting a bicycle, due to the objections of his mother, but eventually he was given one by an uncle who had at one time owned a bicycle repair shop in Latimer Road, White City, not far from the yard used for the filming of Steptoe & Son in later years. This was a pre-war racing machine, which had resided in an attic room of his house in Montrose Crescent since 1933. It was bright red with rust, and the tyres had completely perished. Having pushed this treasure home, he set about completely stripping it down, cleaning and painting it. In the process he learned about ball bearings, and how easy it was to lose them through cracks in the floorboards. The old style 'North Road' drop handlebars were discarded in favour of the more popular French design, new tyres, brakes, saddle and bell were installed, and it was finally ready for a safety inspection prior to granting official permission to ride it to Alperton School each day. The old bike gave good service for a year or two, although it was looked down upon by the proud owners of newer more fashionable models.

The donor of Tony's bike, although in his late seventies, still rode a heavy old style machine which he had built from parts in his shop. Several times a week he would ride to his allotment garden situated alongside the Western Avenue in Perivale. He had been a keen bicycle racer in his younger days, before the turn of the century, and had been refused a taxi driver's licence by the Metropolitan Police, on account of several bicycle speeding convictions dating back to that period. He referred to 'Penny Farthing' machines as 'Ordinaries'. After being knocked off his old growler at the canal bridge in Alperton at age 80 he was finally persuaded to give up cycling.

Derek was more fortunate, graduating earlier from an old upright machine to a brand new Armstrong racing bike, purchased from Sudbury Cycle Works for the sum of 24 pounds.

Purchased 'on the knock' (hire purchase) and partially financed from his paper round earnings, this machine gave many years of good service.

Most of the more common bicycles would sell new for around 20 pounds, a considerable sum in those days, when the average wage for unskilled labour was 10 pounds for a 48 hour working week. Special, made-to-order racing machines, by firms such as Claude Butler of Ealing, would sell for considerably more. On one occasion the authors rode out to High Wycombe to view a specially built model by Rotrax, known as the hundred pound bicycle, with very elaborate, hand painted frame decoration. At the time this amounted to two and a half months pay for an average worker.

In retrospect, the distances ridden by the authors for an evening ride, in the summer, were astonishing by today's standards. Day trips to Brighton and Southend were not unusual, the time to reach Brighton from Wembley being around four and a half hours, with a couple of hours rest on the beach before the return trip.

Cycling clubs were very popular at the time, and every weekend would see large groups of club riders on the major roads. Motor traffic was very light at the time and cycling could be a pleasure. One would also see the occasional speed fanatic, usually with a high ratio fixed wheel and toe-clips, on a sports bike stripped of mudguards, with either one or two aluminium water bottles fitted with a drinking straw, held in carriers fixed to the handlebars. The normal uniform of these speed enthusiasts would be shorts and a sleeveless vest, with the occasional green plastic eyeshade.

A form of road racing banned on public roads was the mass start cycle racing held on Saturday afternoons on the private roads of the industrial estate behind Wembley stadium.

In 1952 and 53, six-day cycle racing returned at the Empire Pool. A banked up wooden track was constructed, and two-man teams alternated over a 24 hour period. In the second year, this was changed to twelve hours. Admission was free during the day, when riders were slowly circling the track, but charged for during the evenings when real racing took place. Riders were able to supplement their income by club sponsored two or three lap sprints.

Although fairly unusual, tandems, and tricycle racing machines would still be seen on the roads in the forties and fifties. These for the most part were survivors from before the war, and were no longer produced by the manufacturers.

Powered bicycles, known as Autocycles were also fairly common, and popular with District Nurses and door to door insurance representatives. In the early fifties several add-on engines appeared on the market, one of these being the Minimotor a small engine mounted on a special rear carrier, which drove the rear tyre by friction. A clutch mechanism mounted on the handlebars would engage or disengage the drive as required.

A similar carrier mounted system known as The Power Pack was less often seen than the Minimotor. Another popular conversion was The Cyclemaster an engine built into the rear wheel. BSA also produced a similar 'in the wheel' mounted engine known as the 'Winged Wheel'. The majority of these little engines were rated at around 25cc capacity, however, the largest was a conversion known as the 'Vincent Firefly', rated at 50cc. The Vincent, like its big brother motorcycles was the most expensive and least common of the add-on engines.

The front fork mounted, friction drive engines, still popular in Holland, were relatively unusual in England. All of these systems called for the more robust working bicycles rather than the lightweight racing types, and a motorcycle driving licence was required to operate all of these powered two wheelers.

Some mention must be made of bicycle Speedway, which became popular with a few young boys who were dirt-track Speedway fans. Oval tracks were cleared on bombsites and areas of waste ground, and races were held using bicycles which were for the most part, salvaged from rubbish dumps, stripped of brakes and mudguards and fitted with wide handlebars fabricated from bent gas pipes. A good time was had by all, although the competitors had to be careful when riding to and from the track, due to the un-roadworthy nature of their machines, which would be sure to draw the unwelcome attention of the police. Eventually adult organizers became involved, leagues were formed, and rules formulated. Phillips actually produced a purpose-made bicycle Speedway machine, which was far beyond the financial reach of 99 percent of the riders. The adult organization and rulemaking was like a poison pill to the pioneers who preferred to do their own thing, and make up their own rules. Although a few league riders went on to become genuine motorcycle Speedway participants, the whole movement had faded into obscurity by the mid fifties.

PUBS IN THE AREA.

A Mild and Bitter, and a Babycham please Landlord .

There used to be twenty pubs in the general area of Wembley, if one includes the area from Stonebridge, on the Harrow Road, through to Sudbury on the Watford road, and from North Wembley to Alperton. With the exception of The Torch, which was built just after the Olympic Games, many of these were relatively new at the outbreak of the war, having been built to service the greatly expanded population on the innumerable estates associated with Metroland, and other housing construction by speculative builders in the general area.

Generally, the drinking habits of the population in the forties and fifties were very conservative compared to the wide variety of drinks consumed today. Men would generally drink draught beer, which was available as Guinness Stout, bitter, light and mild ales, occasionally Old or Burton sold from a barrel at the bar. Beer was generally ordered mixed, a half pint of one with a half pint of another, for example mild & bitter. Lager was unheard of at the time. Some pubs also carried draught cider, drawn from barrels at the bar. Children were not allowed in the bar rooms, and were generally required to wait outside the door, and given a glass of shandy, a mixture of beer and lemonade, to drink. Cider was also considered to be a suitable drink for children, and Tony remembers many occasions when he was given a glass outside the Smugglers Inn at Teignmouth in Devon. At that time, the sweet Devon cider was considerably stronger than any beer available today.

Hard drinkers would take whiskey, either singles or doubles, possibly rum, which was invariably Jamaican or Navy. Bacardi, and other white rums were unknown at the time. Gin was considered to be a drink for women and homosexuals.

It is hard to imagine today, with the wide variety of imported spirits available in every pub, that in the early fifties, the only public bar in England to stock Vodka was opposite the Soviet Embassy in London.

It may also be surprising to some, given the plague of teenage lager louts and binge drinkers found around England today, that the average teenager of the fifties and sixties would rarely hang out in pubs. This was in the main due to shortage of money. Wages were not very high at the time, and drinks were not cheap. Most of the spare cash from each weeks wage packet would go towards hire purchase payments, petrol for the motorbike and the cost of taking a girlfriend to the pictures. Most teenage boys did not start drinking until they were dragged into one of the armed forces for National Service. Even then, the thirty shillings a week, paid to national servicemen would not last long in a pub, so most of the beer they drank was from the NAAFI.

So let's return to the late fifties and go on an imaginary pub-crawl around the twenty pubs in the general area of Wembley, consuming half a pint of beer in each, totalling ten pints by the end of the evening. It should be remembered that the beer was far weaker than that sold today. Transportation would be by either motorbike or a semi derelict 'old banger'. This was before the days of the MOT, which swept most of them from the roads.

Drunken driving was still a serious offence in the fifties, but the sobriety test was generally the ability to walk in a straight line for ten paces, and to be able to pick up a sixpence from the ground. This was not a difficult test to pass, and unless the inebriate was belligerent or staggering drunk, he would usually get off with a warning. The breathalyser changed all that.

We start our pub-crawl at The Harrow Tavern, situated on top of the hill, on the Harrow Road, coming from Stonebridge Park. Another casualty of recent times, this large thirties-style building had a bar which resembled a high-ceiling hotel lobby, with a cold and impersonal atmosphere. It was torn down a few years ago, and replaced by a block of maisonettes.

The next pub on our round is The Greyhound located at the edge of Wembley Triangle. Rebuilt in the early thirties, the building still stands, but its future is in some doubt. When last seen recently, it was boarded up and no longer in business as a pub. In its heyday it was particularly popular with people working in the area of the Triangle for a lunch-time break. One of its more ardent supporters was Arthur Phelps. Its evening regulars would have been from the adjacent Oakington Manor housing estates, who would also use the Harrow Tavern.

We then proceed up Wembley Hill Road, turning left up Dagmar Avenue to The Green Man Hotel, the original Wembley village pub, located on Wembley Hill, opposite the stadium. The present building dates to 1906, and replaced an earlier building. It was a popular stop over for the crowds making their way to and from the evening events in the Wembley Stadium, such as Speedway and greyhound racing.

Returning to the Wembley Hill Road, we continue on our way to The Torch. a nondescript establishment, built across the road from Wembley Park railway station after the time of the 1948 Olympic Games, this pub remains as a monument to the event, but other than this historical aspect, it has nothing whatsoever to recommend it.

We quickly finish our half pints and proceed to the next pub on the crawl.

We then arrive at The Century, a mock-Tudor building at the Wembley Park end of East Lane. Built in 1927, for Metroland, it was a quiet establishment, which was also recently demolished and replaced by a block of flats. May it rest in peace.

Continuing along East Lane, past the GEC works, we turn left into Landover Road to visit The Norfolk Arms. This little pub is a part of old Wembley. The present building dates to around 1860, and at one time had a gymnasium in the rear where prize-fighters were trained. It is a pleasant, quiet establishment today, and can be recognized by a large flag of St. George painted on the end wall of the building next door.

From the Norfolk Arms, back to East Lane, it is a short journey to The Hop Bine. This pub was built around 1871, adjacent to North Wembley railway station. A well attended pub during the War, the building was a well known venue for jazz groups in the fifties and sixties.

At the end of East Lane, turning left again, into the Watford road, we soon arrive at The Mitre. A popular pub for locals in the area, it was always abuzz with conversation. In the late fifties, we were looking for somebody who lived nearby, and stopped at the Mitre to see if he was there. We were accompanied by an eccentric friend on a motorcycle, whose attire consisted of engineers boots, jeans, a broad horizontal striped black and white sweater, leather gauntlets, a dark blue nurses cape and RAF Mk8 goggles, all topped by a black silk top hat. This apparition wandered into the Mitre public bar and stood there looking around to see if our friend was present. On his entry, the buzz of conversation dwindled to silence. Having ascertained that our friend was not present, he walked out of the pub and climbed back on his motorcycle. The silence in the bar was maintained for about fifteen seconds, and then, as if turned on by a switch, the conversation returned at about twice its previous volume.

Continuing along the Watford Road towards Sudbury for about half a mile we come to The Swan, located just before the Harrow Road branches into the Watford Road. Originally this was where the tram lines terminated, although this was later changed when the trams were replaced by trolleybuses in 1936 and a turning circle was built.

Having finished our half pint at The Swan, we continue through Sudbury on the Harrow Road, turning right into Sudbury Heights Avenue, passing over the underground railway, we arrive at the Sudbury Arms Hotel. Another typical Metroland pub, built to serve the estates adjacent to Whitton Avenue, it was located on the intersection of Allendale Road and Sudbury Heights Avenue. Sadly, today, its place has been taken by a block of particularly ugly flats.

Our next port of call is somewhat off the beaten track. Following Sudbury Heights Avenue, one turns left into The Rise, crossing Whitton Avenue into Rosewood Avenue, and Robin Hood way which brings us to Horsenden Lane North. Standing alone in Horsenden Lane, on the edge of the Horsenden Hill Park, The Ballot Box was a relatively quiet but popular pub. Tony recalls draught cider being available there as late as 1961, for ten old pence a pint, or about half the price of a pint of beer. It was a very strong cloudy brew, and could be distinguished from vinegar by reading the label on the barrel. Being popular with those who drank for effect rather than recreation, a good deal of this brew was imbibed by the local labouring classes. As the price of beer went up, and the quality went down, draught cider became more acceptable to the public at large. Because of this price differential, most of the traditional cider producers were finally bought out by the large breweries, and thereafter only a watery, gassy, bottled product was available.

Continuing along Horsenden Lane, we cross the canal, and turn into Bilton Road, which after about a mile, joins Manor Farm Road, entering the Bridgewater Road at Alperton. Turning right, we soon arrive at The Pleasure Boat, opposite the Alperton bus garage.

Built alongside the canal, The Pleasure Boat was a working-mans pub in every sense. Originally popular with the narrow-boat traffic on the canal, in 1851 it offered a passenger boat service to London and back. More recently it benefited from the proximity of several large factories on the opposite bank of the canal. On the canal side of the building was an outside gents toilet, the smell of which rivalled that of the Railway Hotel. It was a short distance over grass to the edge of the canal and there is no doubt that many an unfortunate, 'having drink taken' staggered into the shallow but filthy canal water while en route to the facility.

Since it was the nearest pub to the Bilton Road, it probably drew many of its evening customers from that area, via the canal bridge and Manor Farm Road. It could not be recommended as a place to go for a quiet drink.

Following the Ealing Road, over the canal bridge, we come to The Plough on the left-hand side of the road. This pub, opposite the entrance to Dagenham Motors, had the reputation of being a bit of a rough pub. In its time it was popular with the workers in the local light industrial areas which included Dagenham Motors, Lancia, and Glacier Engineering. Today, it still exists and appears to be prospering under Polish management, and hopefully will continue doing so.

The Pleasure Boat, 2010.
One of the few remaining pubs in the area, it appears to still be prospering.

A little further down the road, on the opposite side, we come to The Royal William. Originally serving the large Carlyon Road estate across the Ealing Road, it was located on the Ealing Road/Hangar Lane transition, adjacent to Alperton Lane. This pub has also been demolished to make way for some other tasteless structure.

We continue our odyssey along the road, which has now become Hangar Lane, and arrive at The Fox & Goose. A popular pub, which catered for the little nest of houses built by speculators in the late thirties comprising Clevely Crescent, St Augustines Avenue, and Priory Gardens. It was a relatively quiet pub, almost possessing a pleasant country atmosphere. Back in the forties, the area behind it was virtually undeveloped. A small lane now known as West Gate, served as a short cut to the Western Avenue, on its way passing the Virol Building, a large white American style structure, which was something of a landmark, being the tallest building in the area. It appeared very modern at the time, but the style of architecture dated to the turn of the century. The old Virol building is long gone, and the whole area has now been given over to industrial development, which extends down to the river Brent. The area on the other side of the river, extending to Alperton Lane, used to be the municipal dump and incinerator, which dominated the area with gigantic piles of ashes, and contributed generously to the pollution of the river. This industrial development no doubt increased the customer base of the Fox & Goose, but must have destroyed its old country pub atmosphere. During the fifties it was the venue of a popular local Jazz band.

We continue along Hangar Lane, turning left at the North Circular Road. About half a mile down on the left, we come to The Abbey Hotel situated before the canal aqueduct and roughly opposite the old Twyford Abbey grounds. It was a large establishment boasting a dance hall and was a popular venue for Rock & Roll in the early sixties. Similar in architectural design to The Royal William, it was torn down by property developers in 1994, before it could become a listed building.

Following the North Circular, past the Ace Café, we turn up Beresford Avenue and branch right into Heather Park Drive, eventually arriving at The Heather Park Hotel. Located opposite a community centre, in the middle of a large private estate, this pub apparently had the reputation of being a rough and rowdy establishment during and after the war.

Having refreshed ourselves at the Heather Park, we follow Mount Pleasant to its end, bringing us to the Ealing Road, and The Alperton Park Hotel. The original pub on this spot was very old, reputed to have been built by a local brick maker during Victorian times. It would have served the long vanished row of small cottages on the other side of the Ealing Road, and labourers from the brick works. The building remains but is no longer a pub.

Following the Ealing Road towards Wembley, we soon arrive at The Chequers on the corner of Stanley Avenue, situated opposite Barclays Bank with the old Alperton Secondary Modern School at the other end of the parade. It was a neighbourhood pub, at one time very busy in the evenings, and very popular with the locals. When last seen in 2010 it was closed and boarded up, and has since been torn down and its site cleared.

And so we finally come to The Railway Hotel and the end of our quest. Standing on the corner of Wembley High Street, and the beginning of Ealing Road, it was an imposing three-storey building, with a fairly large area on the ground floor given over to a Public Bar, and a Saloon Bar. Being a Hotel, there was a dining room for guests, where meals were available to the public during licensing hours. Most of the business was conducted in the Public Bar, which was very popular with itinerant Irish labourers. The establishment boasted a smell of sour beer, which wafted into the street every time the door was opened. This sour smell would even overcome that of the wet fish shop next door in Wembley High Street, where kippers were smoked on the premises. The bare wooden floors, covered by cigarette stubs only lacked the sawdust, which together with gas-lights, would have completed the Victorian atmosphere.

The building cellar area was shared with a gents toilet, accessible by a curving stairway from the pavement of Ealing Road. Apparently rarely cleaned, the stench of urine and vomit emanating from the stairway was enough to turn the stomachs of the more sensitive pedestrians passing by. The toilet also served as an impromptu overnight accommodation for a few of the Irish labourers who for one reason or another had nowhere else to sleep.

There was the occasional drunken fight, but the close proximity of the

Wembley police station was a deterrent to anything serious, and the would be trouble makers were quickly dealt with.

Also at cellar level going down Ealing Road was Eversheds off-licence which enjoyed a symbiotic relationship with the pub. They were agents for Trumans Brewery, and one could obtain quart and pint screw top bottles of Trubrown Ale, Pale Ale, Guiness, and Bulmers Cider. Also available were bottles of cheap fortified wines sold under the name of 'Robin Hood White', and 'Robin Hood Red'. Today this type of brew is generally only drunk by alcoholics, from a bottle concealed in a brown paper bag. Good quality sherry and port were available, drawn from barrels into the customers own containers, but French wines were almost unheard of at that time by the working population. Soda-water siphons could be left to be refilled off the premises. The usual spirits, such as whisky, gin and rum were sold. Also available were certain cocktails such as Pimms Number One, and various liqueurs which would be considered by the average working class drinker of the time to be fit only for poofs and prostitutes.

Lemonade and ginger beer were sold in screw top bottles.

Sometime in the seventies, the old pub suffered the indignity of being transformed into a 'Bernies Inn', a kind of yuppie restaurant, with the old outside gents toilet becoming the entrance to 'The Bistro Bar'. The wisdom of opening a steakhouse in an area with a predominantly Hindu population might be questioned in some quarters - however, the new establishment struggled on for several years before undergoing a further transition better suited to the Asian population.

Situated opposite the old Express Dairy building, where Chaplin Road intersects the Harrow Road, The Fusilier is conveniently placed to cater for the business from the Chaplin Road and Farm Avenue estates.

Although planned before the war, this pub was not built until 1961. Therefore it would not have figured in our 1950s pub crawl.

ENTERTAINMENT

WEMBLEY SPEEDWAY.

Two Four Six Eight, who do we appreciate!

After its last meeting at the onset of WW2, Speedway racing returned to Wembley stadium on 9th May 1946. A crowd of 80,000 watched the Wembley Lions soundly beat Bellevue 50 – 32. So began the golden era of Speedway, and for the next eight years, on Thursday evenings, the Lions would attract audiences of around 75,000 for a league match, and as many as 90,000 for a world championship, or Speedway 'test match' against Australia. Indeed by 1948 the Lions supporters club could boast a worldwide membership of over 60,000.

At 7.45 p.m., the evening's entertainment would start with the sound of *The March of The Gladiators* played loudly over the public address system, to the cheers of the crowd and clatter of wartime gas warning rattles. The Marshals, officials, track graders and St John's Ambulance men marched into the middle of the track. From the Wembley supporters came the cry: "Two Four Six Eight, who do we appreciate? – W.E.M.B.L.E.Y.– Wembley", accompanied by the deafening roar of the machines as the riders rode a slow circuit of the track.

Each race would be run over four laps, a total of 1512 yards, on a cinder track. Later in the fifties this was changed to red shale. Four riders, two from each team, would start from an automatic starting gate. The inside and third position were the favoured positions, and these were alternated between teams for each race. The first rider won three points, the second place, two points, and one point for third place. Riders would be paid start money, and extra for every point scored in the race. A lucky rider obtaining maximum points would go home very well off, by the standards of the day.

Each race would take an average of 78 seconds and the match would total fourteen races up to the interval, during which a variety of items would keep the crowd entertained.

These would include marching bands, stunt-riding, and other acts ,including occasionally a high diving act by a one-legged stunt man known as Peg-Leg Bates. After climbing a ladder up a tall tower, apparently with some difficulty, Peg-Leg would jump from a platform into a small tank of water covered with burning petrol. The resulting splash would extinguish the fire.

The rest of the evening featured star riders from other teams with junior and reserve riders from Wembley, riding two and three lap races.

The crowd would gradually drift away after the interval with the younger enthusiasts having to go to school next day. This would be the chance for the less well off boys to get in free, to watch the second half, as the gates would be open with nobody manning the turnstiles. The hard-core supporters would hang on to the end. At the final match of each season the meeting would end with a massive firework display.

The Speedway racing machines were very basic motorcycles, powered by a 500cc high-compression single cylinder engine, running on Methanol fuel. There were no brakes, and no gearbox, so no neutral gear position, just a throttle and clutch lever on the upturned handlebars. The engines were very simple, with total loss lubrication, similar to the early radial aero engines. The type of oil used was a vegetable based Castor oil blend marketed as Castrol R. The machines carried a small section front tyre and a larger heavier treaded tyre on the rear. Gearing is very important and sprockets are usually changed to suit conditions at the different tracks. The bikes were also without exhaust silencers, simply a straight pipe, which produced an ear splitting noise. The combination of the deafening noise, followed by the distinctive smell of castor oil, was a feature of Speedway racing which has been lost to the present generation. The noise level would go far beyond that acceptable by today's health and safety rules.

Purpose made for the track, only left turns could be made by the Speedway bikes. The very low foot-rest on the right-hand side would have made right hand turns very dangerous. There was no foot rest on the left-hand side of the machine, the rider holding his foot up on the straight parts of the track, and broad-siding into the turn with his foot forward resting his steel shod boot on the track. Pre-war riders and old timers used a different technique known as leg trailing. This was a spectacular style of riding where the rider would lay the machine right over and actually lean on his knee and toe. After the war there were still a few riders practicing this art, to the delight of the crowd.

Spectators standing on the bends where these turns were made would be showered with cinders thrown up by the spinning rear wheels of the riders and quickly learned to cover their eyes either with a hand or by holding the programme in front of their face.

Today this would probably be considered an unacceptable hazard by enthusiastic Health & Safety inspectors, and spectators would probably be excluded from those parts of the stands.

Speedway riders were the pop stars of their day, pursued by fans, who avidly collected autographs and photographs. In 1949 when Tommy Price became world champion, his Rotrax-J.A.P. racing machine, along with the trophy, was exhibited in the window of Zip dry cleaners in Wembley High Road. The pavement was blocked by enthusiastic viewers, and other pedestrians had to walk in the road in order to get past. When Tommy Price retired in 1956 after 21 years with the Lions he was still their number two rider. Indeed most of the stars were not young men, and had ridden pre-war. Ron Johnson, who rode for New Cross, finally gave up in his mid fifties.

Thursday was a day of great excitement for schoolchildren and Speedway fans. From late afternoon, you would see supporter's coaches from the visiting team and Lions supporters from the surrounding districts descending on Wembley. Rosette vendors were in evidence around the stadium entrance, and enterprising local householders would allow their front gardens to be used as bicycle parks for sixpence per machine. It is difficult to realize today with Speedway being a minority sport, just how big it was at that time, and what a source of pride and a morale booster it was to the citizens of Wembley.

On a very wet night on the final meeting of the 1946 season 85,000 fans and a further 20,000 locked outside listening to a commentary over the loudspeakers, saw and heard Bill Kitchen ride the experimental rocket- assisted Speedway bike, designed by Professor Lowe, splutter and fizzle it way around the track,

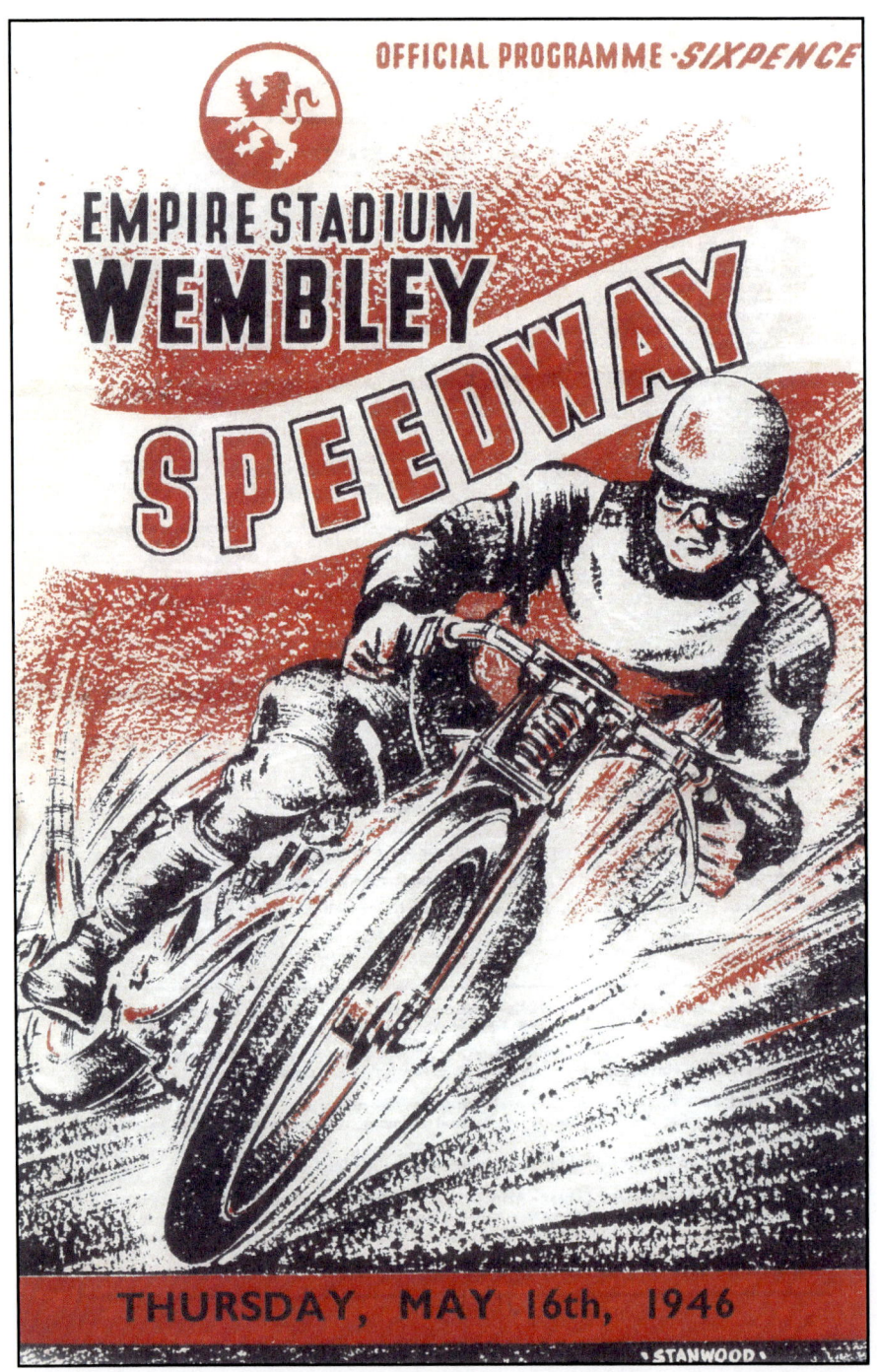

a complete fiasco which consigned it to the rubbish heap, and it was never spoken of again.

The Lions topped the first division league on the return of Speedway after the war, with Tommy Price, winner of the 1946 British riders championship and went on to enjoy eight years as the greatest Speedway team of all time, being top of the first division in 1946, 47, 49, 50, 51, 52, and 53. In 1948, due to the Olympic Games being held at the stadium, most of their fixtures were held at Wimbledon Stadium.

This fact, together with injuries to skipper Bill Kitchen set Wembley back to fourth place in the league for that year.

By 1956, television, falling gates, and a crippling entertainment tax, plus the death of the teams sponsor, Sir Arthur Elvin in February 1957, any hope of Speedway continuing at Wembley was finished. Speedway did return for a couple of seasons in 1970/71, and world championships were held until 1981, but football commitments put paid to any more racing. So ended a post war period of family entertainment that brought excitement and thrills to a war weary population.

THE WEMBLEY LIONS, 1946. Manager Alec Jackson

Bill Kitchen – captain
George Wilks
Tommy Price
Alf Bottoms
Charlie May
Bill Gilbert
Bob Wells
Roy Craighead – reserve
Bronco Wilson – reserve

Bronco Wilson was killed at an away match at Harringay in 1947.

WEMBLEY CINEMAS.

Will you take us in mister? We got our money!

In the days before television, 'going to the pictures' was the most popular form of public entertainment outside the home. The home of course, was dominated by the wireless (radio).

Cinemas offered a world of comfort, glamour, and luxury compared to the drab homes of the 1940s working classes. The cinema offered deep carpets, warmth in the winter, and relative cool in the summer. In Wembley it was possible to visit three different shows a week, plus a Sunday show of re-runs. If one was so inclined it was possible to sit in the warmth from 1 p.m. to 10.30 p.m.

There were three cinemas in the centre of Wembley; The Regal, in Ealing Road, The Majestic (Odeon) Wembley, next door to the General Post Office - and the Wembley Hall, an independent cinema owned and operated by a formidable lady by the name of Nora Thompson. In addition, there was the Odeon cinema in Sudbury. A further cinema, The Capitol, once existed in Empire Way next to the Empire Pool, but was closed early in the war, and the building was converted for use by the Army film unit. After the war it became a stocking factory, and burned down in August 1947. The fire broke out as 70,000 spectators were leaving the stadium after a speedway test match between England and Australia. The police used their new loudspeaker equipped cars to advise the crowd that a fire had broken out, and Derek remembers the announcements asking them to disperse in an orderly manner. Ten fire appliances were required to fight the cinema blaze. At a later date the remains of the building were used by Columbus Dixon, makers of industrial cleaning equipment. The old cinema entrance housed a second-hand bookstore, known to boys as the dirty bookshop, which in addition to having a very fine selection of early science-fiction paperback books, also offered a variety of dubious magazines. These included Spick & Span, Razzle, Health and Efficiency, a nudist publication, and a series of black and white booklets of naked starlets. One of the more popular items was Diana Dors in 3D, sold together with a pair of red & green spectacles for viewing it. In those days, people purchasing such material would be viewed as borderline perverts. Today far more graphic soft-core pornography can be found in the daily newspapers and on what are supposed to be family TV programmes.

A small theatre had been planned in Ealing Road, close to the Regal, in what was later to become Coronet Parade, but due to the war, this was never built. Some time in the fifties, a small public library was built in its place

The Regal Wembley was typical of those built during the golden age of cinema. The multiple glass doors opened into a large and imposing entrance area with two ticket counters. On each side of this foyer, a semi-circular staircase led up to the entrance to the balcony seats; below the stairs, were the entrances to the stalls. Having entered, an usherette with a torch, would check the value of the ticket, and show the patron to a seat in the correct area. Unlike continental cinemas, no tip was expected.

The programme would generally consist of a main feature film, a short second feature, a newsreel, and occasionally a cartoon, with trailers for coming features. The main feature would be shown last. Having paid for a seat, the patrons were not expected to sit and watch endless commercial messages as is the case today. Between features, a girl would circulate selling ice-cream and cigarettes. As a result of rationing, this service was stopped during and for a while after the war.

Smoking was permitted in cinemas, and the flickering beam from the projector could be seen through a rising fog of cigarette smoke from the stall seats. After a visit to any cinema, ones hair and clothes would reek of tobacco.

Whether or not there were seats available, the manager of the Regal would make patrons queue up outside until the current programme ended. This obnoxious individual, apparently took the view that a large crowd waiting might attract an even larger crowd. The more expensive seats were allowed to enter first, while the contemptible one and sixpenny patrons had to wait until the last minute, often in the rain.

During the early part of the war, the Regal suffered some damage when a few stray bombs intended for the factories in Lancelot Road, fell into Montrose Crescent, destroying several houses. Some time after the war, these bombed out houses were demolished, to make a car park at the rear of the cinema.

The Wembley Odeon, although perhaps less imposing from the outside, was a larger hall, which also offered a first-class restaurant at street level and a dance hall on the premises upstairs. With the rising popularity of Rock & Roll, formal ballroom dancing became less popular, and the dance hall closed. It is possible that the hall was used thereafter for wedding receptions in conjunction with the restaurant.

The Wembley Hall cinema, known universally as The Bug-Hutch was an independent operation. Nora Thompson, the owner, ruled it with an iron hand. During the war, while most cinemas would superimpose a slide on the screen warning patrons that an air-raid was in progress, Nora would walk down the centre aisle of the cinema waving her torch, and shouting with a booming voice: "There is an air-raid alert", inviting patrons to leave if they wished. Very few did. In the event of any disturbance during the performance, she would deal with the matter herself, often ejecting the troublemakers into the street.

The Bug-Hutch was a relatively small cinema compared to the Regal and the Majestic, and did not have a balcony. However, taking its programmes from the Gaumont distributors, it was able to offer films which were sometimes more attractive than those of its larger rivals.

Towards the end of the war, the flying bomb which destroyed the adjacent school, blew the roof off of the Bug-Hutch, and it was several months before a temporary corrugated-iron roof helped to put it back into operation. A drawback of this make-shift repair was that the sound of heavy rain on the roof would often be louder than the soundtrack of the film being shown. A further problem was the irresistible lure for young boys to throw heavy stones, and occasional firecrackers onto the relatively low roof from Cecil Avenue, which ran alongside the building.

Despite Nora's formidable reputation, she was a kind-hearted person. Derek, who worked at that time for Phelps Publicity on the Triangle, would deliver her posters for the next week's attractions on his way home. He was always given two complimentary tickets by the good lady.

The cinema programmes normally ended after the pubs closed at 10.30 p.m., so the evening's entertainment might end with a visit to a fish and chip shop, all of which remained open until after the cinemas turned out. Before the last kiss was planted on the face of the heroine and the curtain fell there would be a stampede to exit the cinema before the national anthem was played. Only a few elderly people would remain, together with those unfortunates who had been trampled in the rush.

Both the Odeon and the Regal at different times offered a Saturday morning children's performance, known to the patrons as a Sattadee Matenee. The price of admission was sixpence. In the Odeon, the audience, consisting largely of boys was required to participate in a sing-song before the film performance began. An individual with a piano-accordion would become increasing frustrated when the audience steadfastly refused to join in. Having apparently convinced himself that everybody enjoyed a sing-song, he would soldier on, despite the increasing buzz of conversation and stamping of feet, until his half-hour session ended.

The Regal cinema formed an organization known as the ABC Minors, and had a song which everybody in the audience was supposed to join in before the morning performance started. The films shown at these Saturday morning children's performances were generally 'B' westerns, starring Roy Rogers or the Lone Ranger, and thirties science-fiction serials such as the Buck Rogers series. The occasional Walt Disney or Warner Brothers cartoon was thrown in for good measure.

Going to the cinema on or around Guy Fawkes' Day would always be an adventure, with the certainty that teenage hooligans would set off firecrackers either in the hall or in the rear exit corridors as they were leaving. The firework of choice was generally a Brocks 'Boy Scout Rouser' or 'Atom Smasher'. Unlike today's mild products, a fire cracker of the forties, set off under a dustbin lid, would lift it six feet into the air. On at least one occasion, a sky-rocket was set off from the front seats of the stalls in the Regal.

The British Board of Film Censors issued a certificate for each film before it was allowed to go on to public display. The type of film was designated by a letter: 'U' for universal where children could be admitted without an adult, whilst 'A' for Adult, required children to be accompanied by an adult. 'X' rated films were considered unsuitable for children, due to sexual content. Adults only were to be admitted. 'H' rating was for Horrific content, where again only adults were admitted.

When an 'A' film was being shown, it was not unusual for an adult to be approached outside the cinema by a young person asking "Can you get me in mister?" He had the money for the ticket, but needed an adult to buy it for him. More often than not, the ploy would work. The other ploy used by more adventurous boys, would be to have one of their number buy a ticket, and later, visit the toilet and raise the bar on the emergency exit behind the cinema, so the other boys could sneak in after he had returned to his seat.

The usherettes were not blind to this scheme, and if they noticed a small boy visiting the toilets half way thorough the film, they would catch the others trying to get in.

Up to the fifties it was customary for two members of the St Johns Ambulance Brigade to attend cinema performances. They were not paid for this service, but gained free entry to the performance and were available to attend to any minor medical emergencies which might arise during the film.

There are now no longer any cinemas in Wembley. Either they have been demolished, or the buildings have been turned to other uses. Given the popularity of films and cinemas in India and Pakistan this is perhaps surprising, considering the present dense Asian population of in the area. The availability of rental DVD and cassette films of the Bollywood genre may explain this.

EATING OUT IN WEMBLEY.

Rock and chips with salt and vinegar, and here's my newspaper mate

Wembley was never overburdened by eating establishments. There were tea rooms above the Lyons bakery opposite Wembley railway station, and several small working men's cafes along the Ealing Road, but the most elegant dining room was situated beside the Odeon Majestic as a ground floor annex to the ballroom in the same establishment. However, in general Wembley was not as well served in these matters during and after the war as it is today.

During the war, by government decree, local councils were required to provide communal kitchen centres, to provide 24 hour feeding facilities for emergency service workers and bombed out families. These became known as British Restaurants. There were six such establishments in the area, the first, opening in Kingsbury in December 1941. The largest was situated at the junction of Ealing Road and Wembley High Road. When it opened in September 1942 at a cost of five thousand pounds it was compared by Wembley council and the local press to a West End night-club, a comparison that was clearly ridiculous to anybody who ate there.

The next largest British Restaurant was constructed opposite the Heather Park Hotel, and remains today as a local community centre. A third establishment was started in the Abbey Estate, and this subsequently became the only British Restaurant in the area to consistently show a small profit. Another situated around the junction of East Lane and the Watford Road, in Lincoln Parade was considered to be an eyesore and the subject of much acrimonious correspondence in the local press.

The remaining two facilities in the immediate Wembley area were in Court Parade Sudbury, and Oakington Parade, Tokyngton

Administered by the local council, they were staffed largely by volunteers from organizations such as the WVS; they provided a full three-course meal for one shilling and a penny ha'penny, or a little over five new pence. It was a wonder the Wembley council rejected the proposal that meals should cost two shillings and sixpence, as was the case in many other areas. Perhaps for this reason the restaurants ran consistently at a loss, and the council could not close them down fast enough when the opportunity arose.

The restaurant in Wembley High Road was turned into a labour exchange, and the Heather Park branch became a community centre, which remains open to this day. The Sudbury Court Parade Restaurant closed after only a short time.

Prior to the early sixties in England, it was not customary for food to be served in public houses, other than bags of crisps, which at the time came complete with a little blue paper twist of salt. This of course stimulated the thirst, but did little to eliminate the hunger. The exception to this was the Railway Hotel, which had a dining room for guests, and also served pub customers during licensing hours.

All other tea shops and restaurants had closed their doors by 6 p.m., with the exception of the government operated British Restaurants which remained open 24 hours throughout the war, and the dining rooms beside the Majestic cinema, which may have remained open until 8 p.m.. After this, the only remaining establishments serving food would be the fish and chip shops, or in some other areas of London, the pie & eel shops. At the time, Wembley did not have a pie & eel shop, the nearest being on the Harrow Road at Scrubs Lane, which the authors would cycle to from time to time in the fifties, but the town did have several fish and chip shops, one of which was in the High Street, across the road from the General Post Office. Three others were to be found in Ealing Road and one in Lyon Park Avenue just round the corner from the Heather Park Hotel, but the best by far, was a small establishment known as the Yorkshire Fish Restaurant. This little gem, apart from serving the finest fish & chips in the area, had a number of peculiarities, which set it apart from the others in Wembley. It was situated in Station Grove between Montrose Crescent and the steps leading up to Wembley High Road.

To begin with, the title of restaurant was somewhat pretentious, since there were no tables in the small establishment, and nowhere to sit down. At some time in the past, a travelling salesman had convinced the owner that a UV air ionizer would reduce the cooking smell and clean the air in the shop. In fact the Crooke's tube in the device produced so much ozone, that customer's eyes would be burning and watering before they were ever served. Since the place was very popular, there was always a sizable queue of customers waiting to be served, and each order was cooked fresh.

The apparent owner of the shop was a thin individual with very wavy hair, covering a receding hairline. The waves may have been due to excessive use of Brylcreem, or possibly fat from the fryer. He maintained a bland expression and never spoke to customers. However, the most notable aspect of the premises was the succession of many different young women assistants, all of whom appeared to be heavily pregnant. This situation continued over a period of several years. There was speculation that he procured his assistants from a home for wayward girls, but the matter was never satisfactorily explained.

The fish and chip shops would generally remain open until the cinemas turned out around 11 p.m.. The licensing laws mandated that the pubs would close at 10.30 p.m., so the busiest time would be from 10 p.m. to 11.30 p.m.

As was customary at the time, the fish and chips were fried in pure lard or beef dripping, and the smell of the fish and chips cooking in this type of fat was far more appetizing than the tasteless vegetable oil used today. The fish and chips were served and wrapped in newspaper, and there were no reports of widespread deaths occasioned by toxic elements in the ink contaminating the food.

A bag of chips could be had for sixpence, and many a pupil of the area schools would spend their dinner money at a chip shop rather than partake of the culinary delights offered by the school kitchen.

The remaining fish and chip shops in Wembley were of average quality with little to choose between them other than the distance one would have to walk to get there.

The fish on offer was generally Cod, Haddock, Plaice, Skate, and Rock Salmon, a species of small shark, or dogfish. The northern practice of serving mushy peas had made no headway in the south, and most people would have been revolted by the very idea. Even pickled onions were rare.

The working men's cafes would open in time to catch the night shift workers coming off duty, and close around 2 p.m., after the lunch break. Simple fare was offered, consisting for the most part of fried meals. Sausages made of fifty percent soy flour and fifty percent minced gristle (beef or pork), powdered egg, tea served in large cups or mugs, with saccharine instead of sugar, and bread spread with National Margarine, the same "Dreadful Stuff" satirized by Hilaire Belloc fifty years earlier. The sausages, generally known as sawdust sausages, could be found in tinned form as part of British army rations as late as 1960.

A little off the beaten track there was the Ace Café, a transport drivers restaurant situated on the North Circular Road, close to Stonebridge Park underground station. This establishment remained open 24 hours, and was only closed on Christmas Day.

Towards the end of the forties, milk bars and coffee shops had become popular with teenagers, who, having little money to spend were unable to congregate in Public Houses.

The first of these in Wembley had started as an Ice cream parlour, DeMarco's in Ealing Road, and another Italian establishment in Wembley High Street, between Marks & Spencers and Park Lane.

Later a more typical coffee bar opened in Wembley High Road, in the parade of shops between Park Lane, and the air raid shelters adjacent to the Wembley Timber Yard. This establishment remained open in the evening, until the two nearby cinemas turned out, thereby gaining a large number of late customers.

A less salubrious establishment opened in Sudbury next to the trolley-bus turn around. This coffee bar, known as the Kannibal Pot was favoured by teenagers and the rougher element of the immediate area. This was not a motor-cyclists hang out but was popular with Teddy Boys and best avoided by people of a mild disposition. Certain individuals who later became quite famous in the pop music world used this coffee bar when attending band practice at the hall behind the adjacent Swan Public House.

While a visit to the fish & chip shop was an occasional treat to be looked forward to, the average working class family in the forties and fifties, tended to avoid the more up-market restaurants, generally feeling intimidated in such places, with the several pieces of additional cutlery, and the menu often printed in French. Also the feeling of being looked down upon by the waiters, who although working class themselves, often felt superior to factory workers. This petty class-consciousness gave rise to a snobbish attitude, which thankfully is considerably diminished, even if not altogether eliminated today.

A small middle quality restaurant later opened in Coronet Parade in Ealing Road, opposite Chaplin Road. The Coronet Restaurant was a modest well run establishment where working class families could go for a special treat, without feeling intimidated, however, like most establishments in Wembley, it closed by eight in the evening.

THE WIRELESS.

This is the BBC Home Service. Here is the Nine O'Clock News, and this is Bruce Belfrage reading it.

In the days before television, the main form of live entertainment in the home was 'the wireless'. Which provided news, weather and sport reports, interspersed with music, very popular comedy shows, radio plays and thrillers.

In order to operate a wireless set, a licence was required, available at any post office for ten shillings. In 1946, this fee was raised to one pound, with a TV license costing 2 pounds. Wireless licences remained at 1 pound until 1965, when it was raised to one pound five shillings. With the proliferation of inexpensive transistor portable radios in the early sixties, and the general inclination of the public to refuse to buy a wireless licence, efforts to collect licence fees began to cost more than the revenue gathered, and wireless licenses were finally abolished in 1970.

Meanwhile the television licence had risen to five pounds, and continued to be raised annually to its present level of 142 pounds a year.

During the forties, a wireless set was a big investment for a working family, and many households were still nursing along battery operated sets dating back to the thirties, or even the twenties. It should also be remembered that up to the late forties, about a third of the country was not yet connected to the national grid, and Tony spent his short wartime evacuation to Norfolk in a house with no electricity or piped water. In some towns, many of the houses were still lit by gas, as were the street lights in many parts of Wembley.

These old radios generally required three batteries. The HT battery, usually an Ever Ready Winner, 120 volt, which was about ten inches by eight inches, by 3 inches deep would last a few weeks, depending on how loud and for how long the radio was played. The LT generally consisted of a 2 volt, glass-cased accumulator, which could be recharged, generally at either a radio store or a garage. Most families would have two accumulators, one of which would be on charge while the other was in service. Finally there was the grid bias battery, a 9 volt block with plug points every three volts. Since little or no current was drawn from this battery by the radio, they would last for years. The radio would also require an aerial and an earth connection. A typical aerial at the time might consist of a wire strung from the chimney, to a pole at the bottom of the back garden. The earth connection could either be a rod buried in the ground, or a connection to the main water pipe entering the house.

Safety minded enthusiasts would provide a knife switch to short the aerial to the earth connection when the set was not in use, or during thunderstorms.

For the home-built radio enthusiast, all the technical information required was to be found in a number of publications, most of which were edited by F.J Camm, such as the *News Chronicle Wireless Constructors Encyclopedia*. There were also a number of popular weekly and monthly magazines available during and after the war, Practical Wireless and Wireless World being the most prominent.

Shortly after the war, a large number of small Bakelite-cased, 'Kitchen' radio sets became available on the market. These inexpensive sets, based on a simple American design and originally intended for 115 Volt mains operation, were fitted with a special power cord, known as a line cord, which contained a resistive element to reduce the British 240 Volt power to the correct level. These line cords ran quite hot, and had to be cut to a precise length to do the job required. Replacing them with ordinary power cord would immediately destroy all the valves in the radio. These sets were also available in kit form for home constructors at Smiths of Edgware Road. Mains operated radio sets eliminated the need for batteries, and would generally provide a good reception using the house mains wiring as an aerial. The more expensive commercial radio sets would have short medium and long-wave reception. The dials were generally marked with the major continental radio stations, as well as the BBC. The most popular foreign station was the commercial service of Radio Luxembourg. Although often subject to severe signal fading, Radio Luxembourg could be received over most of England, and carried programming that attracted young people who wanted to listen to the popular music of the day. The directors of the BBC liked to think that they were the arbiters of public taste and refused to allow this type of music, as well as recordings they considered to be in bad taste. Examples of records banned at the time were *The Tomato Calypso, John & Marsha*, by Stan Freeburg, and a number of songs by the popular stage comedian Max Miller. (It can of course be argued that the great majority of

Max Miller's material was undoubtedly in very bad taste.)

Senior positions in the BBC were appointments, and amounted to sinecures for members of the old boys' network. Some of the rules laid down by these vest-pocket mandarins were bizarre, to say the least. For example while the required use of BBC 'Standard English' by announcers can be applauded, the rule requiring radio news readers to be dressed in formal dinner jackets and black bowtie was manifestly absurd.

The arrogance and pomposity of some of these BBC High-ups would sometimes beggar belief. During the war in 1944, the Glen Miller Orchestra was sent to Europe to entertain troops of the AEF in Europe and England. As a courtesy, Glen Miller offered to do a series of broadcasts for the BBC. After only one week, he was called to the office of a senior Director at BBC headquarters. Displaying a total ignorance of the type of music played by Miller, he insisted that the sound level of the music should remain constant during the entire performance; because some listeners in fringe areas had complained that they had difficulty hearing the quieter passages. He apparently equated Glen Miller's orchestra with a military brass band. Glen was unable to comply with this ridiculous request, and without any consideration for the hundreds of thousands of listeners who were not affected by the problem, the Glen Miller broadcasts were abruptly discontinued by the BBC, depriving war weary listeners of the pleasure of hearing the most famous swing band in the world. A few of the more fortunate listeners were still able to hear Glen on the AFN broadcasts to the American Servicemen, which were his primary reason for visiting Europe,

Whether this officious Jack-in-Office would have tried to apply the same rules to the London Symphony Orchestra playing classical symphonies is open to conjecture. He was also apparently unaware that during the war, the power of the BBC transmitters was continuously raised and lowered to prevent the signals from being used by German aircraft as navigation aids. This necessary practice would also seriously affect reception in fringe areas and might well have been the primary cause of the original listeners' complaints.

It must be admitted however, that the BBC generated some outstanding programmes during the war and in the mid-to-late forties. A priceless example was produced by Norman Collins in 1946. This was the daily serial Dick Barton, Special Agent. It was the first serial thriller with the concept of a Special Agent rather than a detective, and with the opening signature tune of *The Devils Gallop* it became an immediate success.

Dick Barton was originally played by Noel Johnson, along with his two sidekicks Snowy White, and Jock Anderson, who spoke with appropriately non-BBC-standard Cockney and Scottish accents which served to place them in the correct social hierarchy for listeners. Nothing comparable to Dick Barton was to appear until Ian Fleming's character James Bond burst upon the world of entertainment in the early sixties.

For the next four years, our hero would battle with power-crazed foreign villains, intent on world domination, tracking down amazing secret weapons, and saving beautiful damsels in distress. Always at the end of each episode, the plucky three would be left in a seemingly impossible situation with no apparent means of escape. This was reminiscent of the Hollywood Flash Gordon movie serials of the thirties, but was more effective because without the visual component, the radio production gave more scope to the listener's imagination.

The program ran Monday to Friday from 6.45 p.m. to 7 p.m., with the omnibus edition on Saturday mornings. During the evening broadcasts the streets would be empty of children. At the height of its popularity the listening audience was estimated to be over fifteen million, and along with Women's Hour it was one of the BBC's two most popular programmes.

It is inevitable that anything popular with the general public will draw criticism from certain quarters. For the most part this came from certain blue nosed clergymen of the Lords Day Observance ilk, and the usual strident 'Looney Left' political minorities, who always feel that society is moving in the wrong direction.

These pressure groups laid a plethora of social ills at the feet of Dick Barton, including, but not limited to, the increase in juvenile delinquency, and falling church attendance.

The BBC, frightened of the monster it had created, caved in under the pressure, and submitted to a censorship list of items to be avoided in future editions of the programmes. These included a ban on any reference to drinking or smoking, although these vices were permitted to a very limited extent in villains. Dick was to have no girlfriends, and the gangsters were to have no molls or mistresses. Violence was to be limited to the occasional clean sock on the jaw. As the list grew, so the audience declined, and the last episode was broadcast in March 1951. No explanation was offered by the critics of Dick Barton for the continued rise in juvenile delinquency and falling church attendances after the series was cancelled.

For a short time the programme was replaced by an uninspiring story of a circus family, named The Daring Dexters. This in its turn was shortly thereafter replaced by The Archers, which had originally been broadcast on one of the BBC regional programmes. It was a story of country folk, which has continued for 60 years to this day, and was beautifully satirized by Tony Hancock on TV in the sixties as The Bowmans.

A list of very popular programmes dating back to the forties would include ITMA (It's that man again) with Tommy Handley, Variety Bandbox with Arthur Askey, Much Binding In the Marsh, starring Richard Murdock and Kenneth Horne, The Charlie Chester Show, Carol Levises Discoveries, and of course, Workers Playtime.

On weekdays for the most part, listeners were subjected to what seemed to be hours of Sandy Macpherson at the theatre organ. The reason for using the organ was that it was cheaper than a live band, and did not incur the royalties payable on records. Other musical programmes would feature various works brass bands, which were probably performing gratis, for the prestige. Workers Playtime was introduced during the war to 'jolly-up' factory workers suffering from fatigue at the end of long shifts.

A number of nondescript bands were used for this service, playing popular songs and melodies of the times. After the war, the programme continued well into the fifties.

Later in the afternoons one could listen to Mrs Dale's Diary, introduced by signature harp music, and generally starting with the phrase "I'm worried about Jim", or 'Womens' Hour', another popular show still being broadcast today, aimed at housewives who would probably be at home to listen to it, having finished their daily shopping and housework in the morning.

'Childrens Hour' would start at 5 p.m., featuring Uncle Mac. One of the more memorable of the children's productions was the Larry the Lamb series. Another great favourite was the boy-detective series, Norman and Henry Bones. Uncle Mac also had a Saturday morning spot with a small repertoire of records, which he would play during the show.

These would inevitably include *The Runaway Train*, *The Laughing Policeman* by Charles Penrose, *A Four Legged Friend*, and the recording of a man who impersonated train noises.

Other favourite evening radio shows going into the fifties would include the immensely popular Goon Show, Around the Horne, with Kenneth Horne and an all-star cast, including Kenneth Williams, and Take it From Here, starring Prof. Jimmy Edwards, and featuring The Glums. Other popular post-war programmes, other than comedy shows, were PC49, Just William, Journey into Space etc.

Perhaps more popular with older listeners was Wilfred Pickles. Originally employed as a BBC announcer using 'Standard English', he hosted a quiz programme using a fake accent reminiscent of George Formby. He could claim an estimated audience of 20 million for his cash prize quiz show Have a Go, and his interminable catch phrases such as "Are yer Courting?" or "Give 'er the money Barney", would grate on the ears of many younger listeners. The pianist on the show was Violet Carson, who much later would play the part of Ena Sharples on the TV series, Coronation Street.

Peter Sellers, playing the part of Wee Sonny MacGregor in the classic Ealing Comedy film *The Naked Truth* probably came closer to the real Pickles character than the BBC would have liked.

On a warm summer, Sunday afternoon, walking down any street in the country, one would probably hear the sound of Two Way Family Favourites, with Cliff Michelmore, and Jean Metcalf, coming through the open windows of the houses, accompanied by the smell of the Sunday dinner cooking.

In all there were over fifty different programmes produced by the BBC in that golden period, many of which were outstanding productions. Space does not permit us to go into greater detail in this little book, however today, the BBC is able to cash in on the wave of old listener's nostalgia by offering CD copies of many of these programmes. Tony owns 24 episodes of The Goon Show, as well as a number of Tony Hancock's timeless classics, still finding them highly entertaining.

Most of the more popular programmes were run in the evenings or weekends, with sports events on Saturday afternoons, and certain comedy programmes repeated on Sunday afternoon.

Also broadcast on Sunday afternoons by Auntie BBC, on the Home Service, was the long-running educational treat, Down Your Way. An outside broadcast van would descend on a town or village such as 'Turnbottom Round'. The interviewer would interview several local rustics or factory girls, about their job or profession, after which they would be invited to choose a record to be played over the air.

Instead of Johnny Ray or the pop songs of the day that one might have expected a girl to choose, the records played were all of a heavy classical or religious nature, more suited to the Third Programme than the Home Service. Although always suspected by the authors, it wasn't until recently it was discovered that the unfortunate interviewees' were shown a list of only a dozen or so pre-selected records from which to choose. The show which was introduced in 1946, was originally hosted by Stewart Macpherson, but in 1947 was taken over by Richard Dimbleby, until he was replaced by Franklin Engelmann in 1955. The programme lingered on in one form or another under a variety of interviewers until 1992.

In the early days of outside broadcasting of football matches the BBC weekly publication, Radio Times, would, in each issue, publish a plan of a football pitch divided up into numbered squares. The match commentator would refer to the position of the players or the ball, for example,

"Tommy Lawton has kicked the ball into square ten, but now the ball has been kicked back to square one". It was thought at the time that this would help the listener to follow the progress of the game more easily, incidentally coining the phrase *back to square one*, which is still used today.

The very important services offered by the BBC included the news bulletins. Prior to WW2, by agreement with newspaper proprietors there were no news bulletins broadcast before 6 p.m., though this was changed during the war. The 6 p.m. evening news was generally followed by the shipping weather forecast and sports report

TELEVISION.

The original TV transmitter at Alexandra Palace went into service in November 1936 with regular programmes. Regarded as a passing fad by the ruling powers at the BBC, it was tolerated as an experiment with no future. The service was closed on the first of September 1939 with the outbreak of WW2. when it was estimated that 20,000 screens went blank when the plug was pulled midway through a Mickey Mouse cartoon.

During the war, the old transmitter was used very effectively to disrupt German navigation aids and communications.

The TV service was restored on a limited basis from 8 p.m. to 10.30 p.m. in mid June 1946, shortly after the TV licence was introduced on 1st June.

The first television sets had a small screen, which produced a dim flickering black and white image, and required about ten minutes to warm up and produce an acceptable picture, while also requiring the room to be partially darkened with curtains drawn during the daylight hours. The service area from Alexander Palace was relatively small, and in many areas a good outside aerial was required. This was the distinctive 'H' aerial, an occasional example of which can still be seen clinging to chimneys, although the old Channel 1 service has been discontinued for some years.

To have such an aerial on the chimney was a great status symbol in the late forties, and many people of a 'Hyacinth Bucket' mentality, who could not afford a TV set, would none the less have an aerial installed to make the neighbours think they owned one. Such was the 'Keeping up with the Jones' mentality of some people at the time.

The old 405-line TV system used in the UK at that time was unfortunately subject to serious interference by car ignition systems, and a large-scale campaign was mounted by the government to persuade car owners to fit suppressors to their spark plugs. The interference would take the form of white spots on the screen and loud clicks on the sound. This problem was avoided by the USA and other latecomers to TV broadcasting, by reversing the polarity of the transmitted video signal. This caused the interference to produce black spots, which were not so noticeable. By also using FM for the sound channel, which was not susceptible to impulse noise, this annoyance was also abated. The problem remained unchanged in the UK until the close of the 405-line black and white service.

The programming in early days was generally live from the studio, or from sports venues. Starting with the opening march, and picture of the Alexandra Palace aerial, the opening announcement would be followed by a children's puppet show, such as Muffin the Mule, Pussy-cat Willum, or The Flowerpot Men The children's programmes would generally be followed by the news. Sports programmes were somewhat limited by the shortage of cameras at the time, the boat race for instance being covered by only two cameras, one at the start and one at the finishing line of the race. Between times viewers would be shown on a studio card display, the progress of the two teams. Two of the early benchmark achievements of BBC television, were the coverage of the Wembley Olympic Games in 1948, and the Coronation of Queen Elizabeth in 1953.

Currys, in Wembley High Road would hold demonstrations of the latest TV sets on Friday evenings after normal closing hours. Derek's father bought an Ecko nine-inch table model for 65 pounds in 1950, a colossal amount of money at the time. The price of a twelve-inch console model would be approaching 100 pounds. Even after the coronation in 1953, when about twenty neighbours crammed into the Addison's sitting room, theirs was still the only TV in the street. In 1955 they bought an add on tuner box which enabled them to view the new ITV commercial channel on band 3, thus giving viewers a choice of two programmes to watch The highlight of the week's viewing was Saturday night with cabaret/variety type shows which might include Café Continental, hosted by Helen Cordet, an old flame of Prince Phillip's navy days in the Mediterranean, and Rooftop Rendezvous introduced by Al Burnett. Some people were so mesmerized by the TV that they would sit for hours and watch the test pattern, broadcast in the weekday afternoons for the benefit of TV dealers, to adjust receivers.

Colour TV was demonstrated at the Radio-Olympia exhibition in the early fifties, but it was not until 1968 that BBC2 transmitted its first regular colour programmes.

The old black and white 405 line service was finally laid to rest in 1985

THE NEW GENERATION

TEENAGERS.

Heavy petting reported among teenagers!

News of The World.

Like many other things that appeared in England after the war, the terms: 'teenager', along with 'juvenile delinquent', were American imports, quickly latched on to by the Sunday newspapers to supplement their sordid tales of fallen scoutmasters, clergymen etc.

Previous to 1950 the terms were not used, and would probably not have been understood. Before this date, there were only schoolchildren and workers. Most working-class children were spat out by the education system at age 14 and found a job in the industrial complexes being rebuilt after the destruction caused by the war. The boys would then have three years of relatively poorly-paid employment before being called up into one of the forces for National Service. Those fortunate enough to be serving an apprenticeship, or attending university, could look forward to a few extra years of freedom before their turn came. Up until the fifties, most teenagers dressed and behaved like their parents, and tended to marry earlier than today. This conformist lifestyle was gradually eroded by post-war austerity and continuing National Service, which ran into the late fifties, and when National Service was increased from eighteen months to two years during the Korean War, it hardly seemed worthwhile to make plans for the future.

The certainty that their lives would be disrupted gave rise to a new attitude which often manifested itself in unruly behaviour, road-racing on motorcycles, and the adoption of a variety of non-conformist dress styles, some of which were American imports and others that were home grown. In the early fifties, an unskilled worker would be earning about ten pounds a week, and a teenager might be earning half that amount, living from hand-to-mouth. Major expenses would include HP payments for the motorbike, petrol, at around five shillings a gallon, taking the girlfriend to the pictures, and in most cases, cigarettes. Coffee, consumed at The Ace Cafe, or in coffee bars would account for the remainder. For most people savings were out of the question. Fortunately, street drugs were unheard of during this period, and the high price of alcoholic drinks prevented public drunkenness and the binge drinking that is so prevalent today. Most people would carry a packed lunch to work, possibly along with a thermos of tea to keep expenses down.

As things slowly improved, and the 48-hour working week was reduced to 40 hours, the opportunity to work overtime put more money in the pockets of teenagers; this was generally spent on clothes of one sort or another which were de-rationed in 1949, or possibly on records of the new music. With the general increase in affluence of teenagers, a whole industry developed to relieve them of their hard-earned money.

The men's clothing shop, Smart Bros, on the corner of Ealing Road and Montrose Crescent, opened in 1950 selling flashy American style clothing, bright shirts with cut-away collars, Hawaiian shirts, T-shirts, which were new at the time, trousers in colours your dad would never have worn, and flashy knitted ties

In 1953/54, the teddy boys made their appearance. A fashion originated in the London financial centre by city clerks, consisting of an Edwardian styled suit with velvet collar and trousers without turn-ups. Was appropriated by the working class lads who exaggerated it to a cult uniform: velvet collared drape jacket almost to the knees, tight drainpipe trousers, heavy black leather or blue suede crepe soled shoes, and a fancy waist-coat with a bootlace or Slim-Jim tie. A teddy boy could spend many pounds at Burtons on a made-to-measure suit cut to his individual taste. These individuals were noted for punch-ups at coffee bars, and generally antisocial behaviour.

After the shorter hemlines and slacks of rationed wartime fashions, girls were attracted to the feminine, more elegant 'New Look' styles of 1949, with waspy waists, and later the felt flared skirts with multiple petticoats. Along with these of course were the seamed nylon stockings with their essential suspender belt. Unlike the almost clinically uninteresting tights of today, the mysteries of girls underwear offered a wonderland of exploration for a red-blooded youth in the dim back row of the cinema. Girdles, corsets, basques, etc. presented countless mysteries to be discovered by an exploring hand.

Blue cotton denim jeans, when they first appeared in the UK, were classed as overalls or work clothes, but after seeing the movies of cowboys and Marlon Brando who all wore tight jeans with four-inch turn-ups, the style became immensely popular in the UK. Derek spent hours on his mum's sewing machine, trying to duplicate the double seam, tapering his jeans down to 15 inch bottoms.

The traditional Jazz scene did see a fashion that was definitely student, college and art school orientated. Known initially as Bohemian, it featured duffel coats, long knitted pullovers, corduroy jackets and trousers, suede chukka boots, and very long scarves, often in university colours, with lots of black eye make-up for the girls, and whispy beards for the boys. This fashion evolved into the beatnik type in the late fifties a pre-hippic era, when nobody we knew took drugs. The devotees of this lifestyle, imported from the US west coast, lit foul smelling joss-sticks and sat around lighted candles in bottles, smoking nothing stronger than Players Weights. They would read the works of Allen Ginsberg and other cult poets of the Beat generation, and they rarely had sex. They were more likely to be the offspring of stockbrokers and merchant bankers than-working class families, rebelling against their parent's money, which enabled them to follow their lifestyle, and which they would of course later inherit.

By the early 1950s, short back and sides haircuts at barbers were out. The new name was Men's Hair Stylists, and the place to go was Tony's at Wembley Park opposite the Fox film studios. Tony specialized in the American hairstyles seen on the movie stars of the day. The most popular was the teddy boys favourite, the D.A., short for Duck's-Arse, or in polite circles District Attorney, where the sides of the hair were cut and combed to the back of the head like the rear end of a duck

Nobody else was cutting hair locally like this and he gained lots of publicity in the local press, and did in fact appear on TV. The price was probably twice that of an ordinary haircut. Later in the fifties he was cutting hair in Julius Caesar style, long before the fashion was adopted by the Beatles. By this time, would-be pop stars were even having their hair dyed. Ten years previously, a youngster emerging from such an establishment, shampooed, blow-dried, and coiffured , would have been ridiculed and proclaimed a 'Nancy Boy'. Such was the new 1956 teenager.

MUSIC.

Now this is the story of the Rock Island line.

Lonnie Donegan

Recorded music had been around since the turn of the century, and most families had a wind up acoustic gramophone using replaceable steel needles. These machines played the single-track 78 r.p.m. shellac records, ten inches for popular music, and generally twelve inches for classical music. Recordings by popular artists, such as Vera Lynn, Bing Crosby, or George Formby would be available for years, and were generally popular with the parents of the new generation. These however, were rejected by the kids in favour of American artists such as Frankie Laine, Guy Mitchell and Johnny Ray. Home grown crooners such as Donald Peers gained some ground with the younger female population, and for a while he had his own radio show.

Band leader and trumpet player Jack Jackson had a popular evening record programme, and could probably lay claim to being the first UK disc jockey, playing and presenting records in a style to appeal more to a younger listener. His program trade mark was the mewing of his cat. The BBC was finally brought to the understanding that this was what a large proportion of their audience wanted to hear

1952 saw the first of the top-ten hit parades, based on sales returns from records shops, the first number 1 being Al Martino, an American Italian ex boxer, who topped the first chart with *Here in my heart* for many weeks.

Saturday afternoons would see the teenagers at the two record stores in Wembley buying the latest records. A ten inch 78 r.p.m.shellac disc cost 5 shillings (25P), or one could purchase a less expensive Decca recording for four shillings and sixpence (22.5P).

Derek Addison's Skiffle Men 1957. Left, Roy Jenkins, Lead guitar, Carlo Little, Drums, Derek, vocals and rhythm guitar, John Manser Bass (The Bass is home made from plywood and two cello strings, an improvement on a tea chest bass!) Using an electric lead guitar and drums, the group was able to perform rock & roll, and pop along with skiffle. This gave the band a degree of performance flexibility which set them apart from other skiffle groups in the area

Derek bought his first long-playing record in 1954, a ten-inch vinyl LP, 33.5 r.p.m. consisting of eight tracks, four on each side costing one pound ten shillings, a 12 inch record with six tracks per side cost two pounds. Seven inch EP records playing at 45 r.p.m. appeared about this time, consisting of four tracks two on each side. These new records could not be played on the old gramophones. Instead, a modern self-contained player and amplifier such as the Dansette, or Regentone Handigram, with a sapphire stylus instead of the old steel needle. This required a considerable investment from the point of view of the teenager and for many of them was an introduction to the magic world of Hire Purchase or 'The Knock'. Messrs Curry's, Stones and MMJ in Wembley High Road were paramount at this form of business, and no doubt sold many of the new machines, most of which were built to run at three speeds and cope with all types of records, with a flip over cartridge containing the microgroove stylus for new recordings, and a larger stylus for 78s. Since some of the 7 inch singles, manufactured for juke box use, were sold without the centre knock-out, a plastic bushing which fitted over the standard record spindle was a required accessory.

By about 1960 the seven inch single vinyl had completely replaced the old ten inch 78 single which had briefly flirted with unbreakable vinyl rather than shellac before fading away altogether

The new teenagers needed to identify with their own music. Not every young person took to the music on the hit parade which was being force fed to them by the burgeoning record industry. One alternative to the standard fare was jazz music, which enjoyed a renaissance in England shortly after the war.

George Webb's Dixeylander's were one of the first British jazz bands playing authentic New Orleans traditional music in London. A trumpet-playing Old Etonian, the late Humphrey Lyttelton played with the band for a while before going on to form his own band.

1948/49 saw Graham Bell's Australian jazz band arrive from down under for a UK tour. This band really caught the attention and enthusiasm of jazz lovers, resulting in a proliferation of jazz clubs in smoky basements and back rooms of pubs all over London. This wave of enthusiasm quickly spread to the suburbs and the provinces. Modern jazz from the American West coast also enjoyed limited popularity, perhaps with more mature audiences. Modern jazz was quite rare in Wembley, being heard in only in one or two pubs such as the Hop Bine and the Norfolk Arms. Traditional jazz was far more popular in the area. Steve Lanes Southern Stompers, with vocalist Pamela Heagran were for many years Friday night residents at the Fox & Goose in Hangar Lane. The Crane River jazz band regularly appeared at Kingsbury swimming baths café. Ken Collyer's New Orleans jazz band played at the British Legion in South Harrow, and at Harrow Art School. Chris Barber's band would appear at Wembley Town Hall in concert with Trevor Williams Jazz Men two or three times a year. There were perhaps a dozen or so other bands doing the circuit of larger pubs and halls in the borough.

During the interval some bands would perform a set of numbers, usually on guitar, banjo bass, and washboard in a fusion of blues, work and folk songs that became labelled skiffle, an American term for a skiffle or rent party. It was customary for poor American blacks to gather for an impromptu party and contribute a small sum of money to help the host with his rent, at which they would bring guitars and make-shift instruments, jug blowing, kazoos and harmonicas. The mood was generally enhanced by plentiful moonshine liquor. The phenomenon of British skiffle started in 1955 when a recording of *Rock Island Line* backed by John Henry was released by Decca as a single, taken from an LP recorded by Chris Barber in 1954. Lonnie Donegan, Barber's banjo player, sang and played guitar on the two recordings along with trombone-playing bandleader Chris Barber, playing double bass, and Beryl Bryden on washboard.

Jack Payne, a grumpy retired band leader, who had a Sunday afternoon record program on the BBC Light Programme, grudgingly played the record two weeks running. It became an overnight hit, not only in this country, but in the USA, where it reached number 1, the first British record to do so.

This unique sound encouraged thousands of would be young singers and musicians to form skiffle groups. Its attraction was due to its simplicity. It only took a guitarist to learn a dozen major chords, a tea chest with a broom handle and string to make a bass, plus a washboard and thimbles, giving the kids a chance to make music that they never had before. Being un-amplified and portable the instruments could be played anywhere. We remember playing on the London Underground, and in recreational parks, or just turning up at a youth club. A few sessions were also played in the car park of the Ace Café.

Trumpet player Ken Collyer who had visited and played with New Orleans musicians while working as a merchant seaman, led the first jazz band in this country to feature a group within a band playing this music, with Ken on vocals and guitar, accompanied by banjo, piano, bass and washboard. Also another local skiffle group worthy of mention was led by banjo player Bob Watson and fellow members of the Southern Stompers band.

The limitations of skiffle music, and the influx of Rock & Roll from the States, plus the newly aquired musical skills of some of the musicians who went on to play popular music, meant by the middle of 1958 this unique and very British sound was over, never to return.

"We don't care what people say, rock & roll is here to stay" sang Danny and the Juniors, and by 1957 it was firmly established in this country. Bill Haley and the Comets toured Britain, unfortunately getting nowhere near Wembley except on the screen of the Regal cinema, with the showcase movie of the band, *Rock Around The Clock*. The event saw the wretched dress-suited manager accompanied by two hired bouncers, pacing up and down the aisles with a look of terror, expecting the seats to be slashed, riots, and dancing in the aisles as had been reported in the press at some other cinemas. The manager's relief after an uneventful week's showing was clearly apparent.

Jerry Lee Lewis was thrown out of the country after only one performance at the Granada Tooting, after the gutter press revealed he had married his thirteen year old cousin. "What's that got to do with his music?" grumbled many of his fans.

Jerry Lee did get to play at the South Harrow British Legion, and a few low key gigs a few years later at the lowest point of his career. By 1960 the Granada Harrow had staged many shows of visiting and home grown bands, including Eddie Cochran and Gene Vincent. It wasn't until 1955 that the Musicians Union allowed American musicians to appear in this country. This boycott dated back to the thirties, when the Musicians Union in the States refused to allow foreign performers to appear.

Derek saw the first UK performance by American musicians, being Louis Armstrong and the All Stars at Earls Court, in exchange for The Ted Heath Band appearing in the States.

There were very few halls that ran Rock & Roll clubs in Wembley. At this time youngsters would have to travel to the Railway Hotel in Wealdstone, to hear the Cyril Davis All Stars, featuring singer Long John Baldry. The Churchill Hall in Kenton was a regular gig for the Johnny Rebs. Cliff Bennett and the Rebel Rousers could also be seen at the two above venues.

The Ritz Ballroom in Kingsbury, although strictly a dance hall, did offer an hour-long spot featuring a Buddy Holly sound-alike group that was very popular. An 83 bus ride to Ealing Broadway would find the Ealing Jazz Club situated underneath the ABC restaurant opposite the tube station. Also nicknamed the 'Moist Hoist Club', owing to rainwater ingress, a tarpaulin was suspended under the ceiling to catch the drips of water. This was the home of Alexis Korner, daddy of the British Blues movement. This club would also see the emergence of the Rolling Stones in the early sixties.

Opposite this club, was a pub called 'The Feathers', where we also remember Country & Western music being played upstairs in the middle-to-late-fifties.

The Oldfield Hotel, Greenford, ran Sunday night dances for many years. Although initially rather formal, we having once been refused admission for wearing cowboy boots and jeans, the venue did go on to become a very popular showcase for up-and-coming groups, and a regular Sunday night out for the kids.

The Abbey Hotel, on the North Circular Road, had a Saturday night dance featuring popular bands like The Flintstones, Joe Brown and the Bruvvers, and Duggee Dee and the Strangers.

In the early sixties the scene started to change. Many clubs opened, but rather than featuring live bands, there was a gradual shift towards recorded music, and they finally became disco's.

Another type of music making its appearance in the fifties was the Calypso and steel band music brought into the country with the first wave of immigrants from the West Indies.

The lyrics of these songs were generally bawdy, often touching on current events. They were generally ignored by the BBC for this reason, although with one notable exception. This being *Cricket Lovely Cricket* written and performed by Lord Kitchner in June 1950 and played almost incessantly by the BBC for the rest of the summer of that year. Other classics, such as the *Tomato Calypso* by The Charmer, and *The Big Bamboo*, by The Duke of Iron were banned outright. There were no live Calypso venues in the Wembley area, the nearest large group of West Indians being concentrated in the areas of Harlesden, Kensal Green and Notting Hill.

CAR OWNERSHIP.

So who do you think you are lad, Stirling Moss?

Sarcastic remark made by traffic policemen when stopping young drivers for speeding.

For people accustomed to today's huge volume of traffic on the Harrow Road, the period during and shortly after the war would have seemed like an era of peace and tranquillity.

Tony, living as he did at 583 Harrow Road, next to the fire station can clearly recall that in the evenings, the only traffic seemed to be the occasional trolleybus whispering past. Even the sound of the district nurse passing on her autocycle would be heard inside the house, and on a late summer evening, relaxing in the back garden, the regular tinkle of coal trucks being marshalled in the LMS yards at Stonebridge, mingled with the distant sound of aero engines running up at Northolt aerodrome were the only sounds to be heard. Derek, walking home in the evening after visiting Tony in 1950, can recall walking in the middle of Harrow Road, to the entrance of Barham Park at Linthorp Avenue, without seeing a single vehicle of any kind.

Probably the noisiest things in the evenings were the big Scammell articulated trucks from the United Dairies depot at Scrubs Lane, Harlesden. These would pass through Wembley around 6 p.m. each day, and would occasionally backfire when changing gears, sounding like a cannon being fired in the High Road. Today, the continuous roar of traffic 24 hours a day is a fact of modern life.

From the end of the war until the fifties cars were generally owned by the privileged few and vehicles that came within the price range of the working classes, would need an owner possessed of mechanical skills to keep it running. Tyres often run down to the canvas, petrol was purchased sparingly at one or two gallons at a time, and road tax was always 'in the post' if questioned by the police. Mandatory insurance could be obtained from Pratts of Hillingdon, an insurance broker who would arrange to insure almost anything, remained open until 8 p.m. every evening for the convenience of customers, and would issue an immediate cover note. There were however some exceptions. Certain older cars would require a mechanics report before insurance could be issued. This, in the days before the government annual MOT test sent many a poor old banger to the breakers yard. Although negligible by today's standards, the cost of the insurance was a serious financial burden to the aspiring young car owner. Inevitably, sacrifices had to be made in other directions to cover the costs. Tony, running a 1930 Sunbeam-16 in the late fifties, was forced to start the engine with the hand crank, being unable to afford a new battery to operate the self starter. He also learned how to remove a tyre with levers to repair punctures, and to 'tread' it back on the wheel afterwards. A friend, running a 1929 Lagonda also had to use the hand crank, due to a faulty starter motor, which would cost too much to repair.

Although Jet petrol was available at certain garages for as little as four shillings a gallon, many young drivers resorted to mixing in a portion of paraffin heating oil with the petrol to eke it out. The white smoke and unmistakable smell of the paraffin from the exhaust would inevitably attract the attention of the police and a stiff fine would result. Other perhaps more dangerous practices to save petrol included disengaging the engine, and freewheeling down hills.

Aside from financial considerations, the greatest obstacle to car ownership was the problem of obtaining a driver's licence. On a motorcycle, a learner could ride solo, but in a car, a licensed passenger and an L plate were required. For most young people it was a Catch-22 situation. They might well be able to afford an old banger, but very few friends had a full driving license, and to drive solo without L plates was to risk a nasty fine if caught. None the less, many young men took the risk, and Derek, who having sold his motorcycle was well ahead of the pack in car ownership, drove his 20-year-old Morgan two-seater sports car, and later a Standard Vanguard, on a provisional licence for two years until finally passing his driving test. He was lucky, and never got caught by the police. At that time a provisional licence could be renewed indefinitely without having to take a test.

Naturally, many young ladies found the passenger seat in his car far more agreeable than the pillion seat on a motorbike.

Some people were able get driving licences while doing National Service, but it usually came with a price. While serving in Germany, the RAF offered free driving lessons to anybody who would volunteer. Tony having a cautious and suspicious nature took the trouble to discover that the RAF license was only valid for service vehicles in Germany, and not legal in the UK, so declined to volunteer. He was thus able to enjoy quiet weekends in the NAAFI, while the eager volunteers were sent on practice convoy duties around the German countryside.

Tony got his full driving licence only after leaving the RAF, by spending his RAF reserve pay at the British School of Motoring. Having failed his first driving test, he passed the second, and as the first of his group of friends to become Legal, was much in demand as a front seat passenger.

Tony also had the advantage of having three older brothers and a cousin at home, all of whom were drivers. The cousin had a pre war Ford Ten, which had survived the war in a locked garage, and somehow avoided the government requisition of its tyres. The official who came searching for the car was sent away with a flea in his ear, and the suggestion that he would look a lot better wearing a uniform, by an indignant aunt.

This car was put back on the road as early as 1946. In 1947, Tony's brothers purchased a derelict Wolseley Hornet Special sports car and restored it, later trading it in for a burned out Jaguar 1.5 litre saloon car, which they also restored.

For several years after the war, new cars were very hard to find, and generally reserved for special needs customers such as doctors. The majority of the remainder were exported.

It was not until the early fifties that new cars became generally available, with cheaper models such as the Austin A30 and A35, the Standard 8, and the Morris Minor, and the Ford 100E series such as the Anglia, the Prefect, and the Popular, with its pre-war body style, appearing on the highways. More expensive models such as the Ford Zephyr 6, and the larger Vauxhall Velox models were less common. At the time, the annual road tax was determined by the engine capacity of the vehicle, and larger-engined cars were not popular. Second-hand cars such as a 50 horsepower Rolls Royce, and the larger pre-war American cars, could be found for as little as fifty pounds, but nobody wanted them.

Perhaps one of the more sought-after second-hand cars was the pre-war Austin Seven, and many of these little gems could still be seen on the roads until the MOT swept most of them away.

Generally speaking, many of the British cars produced after the war were of poor quality, and inclined to rust. This was particularly the case with Vauxhall products, which were in many cases found to be suffering from under-body rust before they even left the showrooms, and after three years on the road, the doorsills resembled Brussels lace.

A large number of 'New' cars required a reconditioned engine after only 50,000 miles.

This indifference to quality, combined with union intransigence, and the management perception that they had a captive market, led to the decline and fall of the British car industry over the next few decades.

At a time when the average weekly wage was around ten pounds a week, the Ford car workers at Dagenham were averaging 25 pounds a week, and were constantly on strike over petty issues. A similar situation existed in the car-producing centres of the Midlands. Meanwhile, even beyond the sixties, the cost of a British-made car in the UK could be as much as thirty percent higher than the same model sold in Europe. This was due to price fixing by the car producers and distributors who apparently thought that the wartime take it or leave it attitude could be maintained forever.

In 1958, Derek became the first car owner in Farm Avenue, with his second hand Morgan 4/4. The following year his father purchased a two-year-old black Ford Prefect, which became affectionately named 'The Black Flash'. Although there were several motorcycle combinations in Farm Avenue, these two cars were alone in the street for many months after they were acquired. Gradually however, as things improved, and more and more cars became available, particularly with the launching of the Austin and Morris Mini series, and the classic Morris 1000, car ownership expanded dramatically, and polishing the car replaced mowing the lawn as a primary Sunday occupation in the UK.

An alternative to full-sized cars appeared in May 1948 when the first Bond Mk A - Minicar was produced. The first prototype, actually built in the attic above the inventor's workshop, was a very crude machine. The body was constructed of aluminium and there were two seats. The two rear wheels were unsprung, and relied on the soft under-inflated tyres to make the ride easier. The engine was a Villiers 122cc two stroke motorcycle engine, driving the steerable front wheel via a three speed gearbox. There was no reverse gear. The steering arrangement was a crude cable and bobbin assembly, acting on the front forks to which the engine was fastened. The engine was started by lifting the front hood and operating a motorcycle type kick-start. The inventor claimed 100 m.p.g.at 30 m.p.h. The name Bond was retained when the inventor was bought out by Sharps Commercials and full production on the Mk A began early in 1949. Over the years changes and improvements were made in the design, the Mk C being introduced in 1953.

By this time the engine size had increased to 197cc and the m.p.g. reduced to 85-90.

In 1953 competition appeared in the form of the Reliant Regal, a similar but somewhat more luxurious three-wheel vehicle, with a 750cc overhead valve engine. Reliant also produced a van version of their product.

In the late fifties, a number of so-called Bubble Cars appeared on the British market.

Two of these from Germany were the Messerschmitt KR175, resembling an aircraft fuselage with two seats in tandem, and the Heinkel Cabine, with a front opening door, produced in the UK under license as the Trojan 200. Other bubble cars were produced in the UK by Reliant, and the Peel Company in the Isle of Man, which produced the Trident. Another front-opening model was the BMW product, made under licence to the Italian Issetta Company with front-opening door and side-by-side seats. Where normally the Issetta had double rear wheels, those sold in the UK had a single rear wheel enabling it to be registered as a motorcycle, thus reducing the road tax. However, to be registered as a motorcycle, the reverse gear had to be disabled. This also enabled the owner to drive on a provisional motorcycle license without a licensed passenger. The lack of a reverse gear could lead to problems for anybody who inadvertently parked facing a wall and was consequently unable to open the front door. We know of one case where this happened and the driver spent the whole night in his bubble car, before a passer-by pushed him away from the wall in the morning.

Interest in these various pseudo motorcars diminished when the Austin and Morris Minis became available, along with the Hillman Imp. These high-performance little cars offered everything that was lacking in the three-wheelers and bubble cars.

More and more foreign cars appeared in the UK as time went on, the most notable being the ubiquitous Volkswagen Beetle, which despite its shortcomings of cramped cabin and small luggage space, and some would say ugly design, was probably one of the most reliable cars ever produced.

The French, apparently in an effort to outdo the Germans in making an ugly car, produced the Citroen 2CV, which never became popular in England, and as much as anything, resembled a corrugated iron shed on wheels. Japanese cars were yet to make an appearance.

There was a period in the fifties, when GT-style fibreglass bodies became available which could be fitted on to the chassis of old 100E Fords, or pre war Austin 7 cars. These conversions usually included rebuilding and souping-up the engine. The work required a good deal of expertise and a garage, so very few were really successful. A possible exception was the Lotus conversion kit for the Austin 7. This was the beginning of Lotus Cars, which went on to become leaders in the car-racing world.

Ex military vehicles were very popular in some quarters. A few ex WW2 Jeeps were sold in the UK, but were left-hand drive and finding spares was a problem, not to mention relatively high petrol consumption. When the Rover Car Company started production of the Land Rover series in 1948 they were greatly sought after, most of them going for export or to the military. The aluminium bodywork was a result of post war shortages of sheet steel, but proved to be a priceless selling point for Rover. An Austin attempt to jump on the bandwagon produced the Champ, a good number of which were sold to the MOD fitted with a Rolls Royce engine. When these became available as Army Surplus, the Rolls engine was removed and replaced by an Austin unit. MOD surplus Land Rovers sold for around 250 Pounds in 1960, with the Champ selling for considerably less. At the same time, a brand new Austin Minivan sold for only 450 Pounds.

CAR ACCESSORIES.

With car ownership becoming almost universal, the market for accessories expanded considerably. Apart from cosmetic additions, such as sun visors, and white stripes, which certain car owners seemed to think made their car go faster, some other accessories, such as fog lights and oil pressure meters did in fact serve a useful purpose. For the brainless few, there were sets of Maserati air horns, which could be programmed to play a silly tune, and disturb the entire neighbourhood. One of the more useful of these noise-makers was a particularly loud and high pitched wolf whistle, driven from the inlet manifold vacuum. This accessory had the effect of clearing stray dogs from the road a good distance ahead of the car, and no doubt saved many from being run over.

More expensive modifications for those of a mechanical bent, were twin carburettor manifold kits, and straight through (Glass-Pack) silencers, the first of which were frowned upon by the motor insurance companies, and the second by the police, for 'Uttering excessive noise'.

In the early sixties Tony owned a Hillman Minx family saloon car, which had been modified by the Jack Brabham racing firm. This made the innocent looking car, normally capable of 75 m.p.h., into a 115 m.p.h. surprise for Mini-

Cooper owners, who were fond of fast acceleration away from traffic lights. The original exhaust system had been removed and replaced by a twin pipe system exhausting (illegally) under the front passenger door. The twin pipes would crackle and bang when running downhill, often producing flames as long as two feet. These cars unfortunately were expensive and troublesome to maintain, and Tony finally replaced it with a second-hand Austin Minivan, which gave many years of good service.

OPEN 24 HOURS. (Except for Xmas day)

The Ton-Up kids creed - live fast love hard die young.

Today magazine January 14, 1961

The Ace Café started its life in 1938 as a transport drivers' restaurant on what at the time was a main route intended to divert heavy traffic around London rather than through the centre of the city. By English standards at the time, the new road with two lanes in each direction was a superhighway. At the time, the main trunk roads such as the A1 and the A5 had scarcely been improved, other than by re-surfacing, since they were built by the Romans. Until the M1 was constructed the North Circular remained possibly one of the most modern roads in the country. It must be said that it was far more effective as a bypass route around London than its modern day counterpart, the M25. At least the traffic was moving at that time.

In the early thirties, in answer to a question in parliament by Sir Oswald Mosley, as to why Great Britain could not build a road system comparable to the Autobahn network in Germany, Herbert Morrison, the Minister of Transport, replied that the existing road system in the country was perfectly adequate for the foreseeable future. While this might have been true in the time of Queen Victoria, when only horse drawn vehicles and a few early bicycles had to be considered, at the time the question was asked, it demonstrated a singular lack of imagination on the part of the government. Unfortunately, this type of political thinking was alive and well as late as 1959, when Ernest Marples, who had no driving licence was appointed as an equally incompetent Minister of Transport.

A number of other major road projects were also completed around Greater London in the late thirties. These included the Western Avenue, between White City and Uxbridge, and the Watford Bypass, which had its own transport café, The Busy Bee. This also became a favourite gathering place for motorcyclists in the post-war period, but was never as popular as the Ace.

The original Ace Café was bombed in 1940. A temporary building was erected to carry on trading until it was completely rebuilt in 1949.

By the early fifties, the economic situation was slowly improving, and the dream of a second-hand motorcycle became realisable to many young men seeking excitement in an otherwise drab and boring post-war society. At best, the average wage for a school leaver would be less than five pounds a week. However, an old motorbike could be found for as little as ten pounds. Many of these were in very poor condition, and the owners quickly became quite useful mechanics as a result of having to do their own repairs.

In the days long before the MOT tests, a great many unsafe vehicles were in regular use.

A provisional driving licence was available at age 16, with the proviso that a learner plate be affixed to the front and rear of the motorbike. In addition, the rider was not allowed to carry unlicensed pillion passengers until he had passed his driving test.

At the same time, coffee bars became very popular with teenagers in the UK who used to meet in them in the evenings. These establishments would normally close around 10 p.m., whereas transport drivers cafés remained open for 24 hours. It is therefore not surprising that the newly mobilized teenagers would gather at such places. With little money to spend it was possible to make a mug of coffee last for hours, and the parking area of establishments like the Ace would remain busy until the small hours of the morning.

By the fifties and early sixties the Ace had become a Mecca for motorcyclists of every description, and at its peak, there would be well over a hundred machines parked outside every evening.

Malcome Edgington and Derek, on his BSA Clubmans Gold Star at the First Ace Café reunion in 1994 Photo courtesy of Patrick Goslin, Classic Bike

The provender on offer was the usual lorry driver's fare, consisting largely of sausage and bacon sandwiches and steak & kidney pies served together with large mugs of hot tea or sweet milky coffee. Also on the menu, was a particularly unpleasant combination of offal, soy flour and grease, which at the time passed as a hamburger and bore a marked similarity to the equally unpleasant product sold at that time by the Wimpy chain of restaurants.

Since the motorcyclists generally arrived after 6 p.m. when there were very few lorries stopping, the Ace enjoyed the best of both worlds and business boomed.

During the golden years, the Ace car park opened directly on to the North Circular Road which was much narrower than today. Across the road opposite the café was a huge pile of rubble, which extended up the road as far as the canal viaduct, and came from bomb damaged buildings in Hendon. The first of the 'Seven Arches' was directly alongside Beresford Avenue which also entered directly on to the North Circular. All of this has changed today, with the demolition of some of the railway arches, and the construction of slip roads, which have no direct access to the main road.

RECORD RACING.

In the fifties recorded pop music was becoming increasingly popular with teenagers. However, in order to hear pop music loudly you had to go to fairgrounds or establishments where juke-boxes played. Most of these at the time were in coffee bars, where the management would not always welcome motorcyclists. The Ace welcomed all comers and had a particularly loud jukebox, loaded with the very latest recordings.

This jukebox was the foundation of the 'café racer' legends, which have become very popular with the modern day motorcycle fans. These seem to be for the most part, solicitor's clerks and mid-level management Yuppies, who have as much in common with the original working class bikers, as chalk has to cheese. The motorcycles ridden by these wannabees are generally top-of-the-line Japanese machines and

American Harley Davidson models, which commonly cost more than a small car. Although they can be very fast by virtue of their relatively large engines, their ability to corner at high speed is somewhat questionable. During the heyday of the racers, the stretch of the North Circular Road between Hangar Lane and Staples Corner, became known as 'the four mile racetrack'. The only obstructions in the road in the early fifties, were the traffic lights at the Harrow Road in Stonebridge Park, and the roundabout known as Neasden Circle. Riders coming from the direction of Ealing would pass the Ace at high speed, making the maximum amount of noise while passing under the brick railway arches, which would magnify the sound. They would then turn around at Neasden, and return to the Café.

Neasden Circle was the turning point for the record racers. It was about three miles distant from the Ace. The aim of the racers was to put a record on the jukebox, and make it around Neasden circle and back before the record finished. Since the average record lasted for about three minutes, the round trip had to be accomplished at speeds in excess of the magic 'Ton' or 100 m.p.h. The traffic was fairly light in the evenings, and the road was more or less straight until the bend at the iron railway bridge a short distance before the Neasden circle. This was where most of the fatalities occurred, with riders who were travelling too fast to make the bend hitting the chain link fence dividing the road. The fence would act like a trampoline, and on one occasion, an accident ambulance driver operating out of Wembley fire station, (who happened to be Tony's older brother), recovered the body of an unfortunate racer over two hundred feet from his wrecked machine.

In the early days the road had no speed limit, so technically no law would be broken. Around 1960 a 40 m.p.h. speed limit was imposed, supposedly as a result of the number of deaths and injuries suffered by motorcyclists. This in fact did nothing to curb the racers, who stood little chance of actually being caught for speeding. The machines used by police motorcyclists at the time were Triumph 500cc Speed Twins, which could never hope to catch the average Norton or Triumph racer, and it was not until the introduction of the Daimler Dart sports car to the police stables that things changed. This car, with a V12 Daimler engine, tuned by Jaguar racing specialists, was capable of speeds approaching 170 m.p.h., and could out-accelerate most motorcycles at the time. However they were expensive, and prone to engine fires, which would quickly spread to the fibreglass bodywork.

THE POLICE.

Up to a point, the police were content to leave the Ace alone. Since it was in an industrial area, there was no problem with the noise, and it was a convenient place to look for people who had committed some offence elsewhere, knowing they would be sure to turn up at the Ace sooner or later. So far as speeding was concerned, the North Circular Road was de-restricted in the early days, and as long as the riders were not 'Driving without due care and attention' or 'Driving dangerously' they were committing no offence.

There was no alcohol available at the Ace and it was considered preferable by the authorities, to have riders concentrated in one place, rather than spread out around pubs in the area.

Periodically each evening a squad car from Wembley would visit the café to show the flag, but generally speaking there was very little hooliganism to draw the attention of The Old Bill.

Less fortunate were the young constables who were sent to try to locate and possibly arrest certain individuals. At the time, individual police officers were provided with a small, almost silent, water-cooled Velocette motorcycle, affectionately known as a 'Noddy' bike, after the children's TV puppet character. On a number of occasions these lone officers left their Noddy bike outside while they went into the Ace to seek their quarry. On returning they would find the machine had vanished. In their absence it had been picked up by a group of burly bikers and thrown over the five-foot concrete wall behind the café car park, into the river Brent. This wall no longer exists, since about twelve feet of the Ace car park was chopped off in order to construct an access ramp to the riverbed, and the original wall was replaced by a lower fence. Rumour has it that the remains of these Noddy bikes were found by workers constructing this ramp. While this behaviour would certainly be viewed as criminal vandalism by the police, there was never any violence or horseplay with the officer concerned. It was enough that he had to suffer the embarrassment of calling for transport back to the police station and process the mass of paperwork occasioned by the loss of his machine.

THE BIKES.

In the early fifties, an astonishing variety of motorcycles would show up at the Ace, from pre-war racing machines, to big old sloggers, such as the 650cc single cylinder Panther, which was primarily intended as a sidecar model. Most of these 1930s bikes had been laid up during the war. Very few sidecar combinations would be seen, as these were generally operated by family men with other things to do in the evenings.

New machines were hard to come by, due to the government's export drive for ten years after the war ended, so the enthusiasts had to make do with what they could get.

As time passed and the economic situation eased, new models became available to those who could raise the deposit required to buy one 'on the knock'.

The UK market in those days was dominated by Triumph, Norton, BSA, AJS, and Matchless. HRD Vincents, or even the 500cc Comets were still out of the financial reach of most of the youthful riders, as were the German BMW models. A few other types were also available, which have long since vanished from the scene: the Aerial Four Square, a 1000cc machine intended for sidecar service, but which, when ridden solo was capable of remarkable acceleration; the Douglas, an elegant machine with a flat twin engine and the larger Velocette models. Other makes, less popular with younger riders, such as the Royal Enfield (still produced in India) also became available.

It was relatively unusual to see an American-made machine at the Ace. The 750cc Harley Davidson machines sold off as army surplus at the end of the war were usually fitted with a sidecar by the purchaser. While comfortable to ride compared to the British motorcycles, they were also relatively slow and cumbersome, so were not popular with young riders. A notable exception was a diminutive American woman who would show up at the Ace from time to time, riding a new 1200cc Harley Hydraglide. She attracted a good deal of attention from the regulars, who for some reason seemed unable to kick start her machine. The probable reason for this was the geared-down kick start on the Harley Davidson, which required a somewhat different technique to the British bikes. She probably came from the US base at Ruislip, but we never found out for certain.

The machine that finally came to epitomize the café racers was a hybrid, consisting of a Triumph engine, mounted in a Norton 'Featherbed' frame. It had long been recognized that nothing could lay over on a fast bend better than a Norton, but the Triumph engine had the edge on top speed. These hybrids, known as Tritons can still be found, mainly in the hands of collectors. Many of them had a toggle switch fitted behind the rider's seat, enabling him to switch off the rear lights when being chased by the police at night. But for the serious would-be racer, the ultimate goal was the BSA Gold Star, a racing motorcycle that came fitted with just enough equipment to make it road legal. With its high ratio gearbox and racing carburettor it was a difficult bike to ride in traffic, the rider having to slip the clutch in first gear up to 30 m.p.h. A lot of future stars of motorcycle racing started their careers on these fast singles. It was also a particularly noisy machine with the bare minimum of silencer in the exhaust system for it to comply with the law.

THE CLOBBER.

The clothing worn by the riders, evolved over time as the relative affluence of the country's economy changed. In the early days, a rag tag assortment of warm clothing was worn, much of it being government surplus, probably purchased from Millets

Popular items included ex-RAF flying boots and sheepskin Irving jackets, leather gauntlets with silk under gloves, and the ubiquitous Mk8 pilot's goggles. Also popular at the time were the sleeveless ex-army, leather drivers jackets, and knitted roll neck sweaters, the ex-Navy variety being particularly favoured. Later, more and more purpose-made motorcycle leather outfits appeared, and it was not unusual to see riders sporting a full set of racing leathers with leather boots to match.

After the Marlon Brando epic, *The Wild One* enjoyed limited circulation in the UK in 1953, ex-US Army and Navy black leather jackets became popular. Some riders were unwise enough to paint skull and crossbones, or some other such motif on the back of these jackets, and quickly learned that this was a sure and certain way to be frequently stopped by the police.

Crash helmets were not compulsory for motorcyclists until the 1970s and many riders didn't bother particularly in the summer months. In the early fifties, some riders would, for protection wear the corker skidlid, but discarded them for the new American style jet helmets when it was found that the peak fitted to these early models would more often than not break the nose of the wearer in the event of an accident. The more sporting riders chose the Cromwell racing helmet as worn by the track and road racing stars of the day. Some of the lone old-timers might be found wearing an ex-army half-football dispatch riders helmet.

Although the police had started using the original Skidlid crash helmets, it was soon found that the peak was a liability and they were replaced by an improved model.

THE DEMISE OF THE ACE.

By 1969, the motorways were taking the majority of the heavy goods traffic away from the traditional routes, and most of the old long- standing transport cafes closed down. This factor, combined with the fact that the increased affluence of the times enabled young people to acquire small cars such as BMC Minis (which were in any case, much more acceptable than motorbikes to the parents of girlfriends), caused patronage of the Ace to diminish rapidly. A further problem was the emergence of a new class of rider known as Rockers. These individuals generally formed gangs, attracting the further attention of the police, who often found evidence of drugs being sold both inside and outside the premises. The final straw perhaps was a sensation-seeking expose, by a TV news reporter resulting in questions being asked in Parliament. As a result of this downward turn, the Café closed in 1969 and was taken over by a tyre company, 'Just Tyres', which remained in business until 2001, when after seven years of untiring effort, a man with a vision, former police officer Mark Wilsmore acquired the premises, and re-opened its doors as the new Ace Café.

Although every effort has been made to recapture the original atmosphere, old-timers returning for a visit are struck by the present- day cleanliness of the new Ace, and the fine quality of the food available. Such are modern times. Any effort to restore the original squalor of the dining room or the 1950s bill of fare would surely bring down the unwelcome scrutiny of public health inspectors and the establishment would be closed down again, perhaps forever.

Today the resurrected Ace has become the venue for a wide variety of popular rallies and entertainments, and stands a good chance of being listed as an historical site. Even the presence of scooters is tolerated in the car park, which is perhaps a sign that the Ace Café of yesteryear is gone, never to return. Today, visiting 'Mods' on scooters can rest assured that their machines will not go the way of the Police Noddy bikes, over the wall into the Brent, as they might well have done during the heyday of the Ace.

ACKNOWLEGEMENTS

The Authors of this book would like to thank Moirag Kane and Ken Kirkman, for their help and encouragement in the publication of this book.

Particular assistance was also provided by Kate Jarman, archivist at Brent archives, Willesden,

Other valuable sources of information include:

'A History of Wembley', Edited by G. Hewlet, published by Brent Library service 1979

'Municipal Housing Handbook', Published by the borough of Wembley 1952.

'Wembley Official Guide' Published by G.W. May Ltd. 1939.

'Wembley presents 25 years of sport'. Published by Wembley Stadium Ltd. 1948

2010 photographs and cover pictures of the Ace by lisrockphoto.com

The opinions expressed in this book are our own